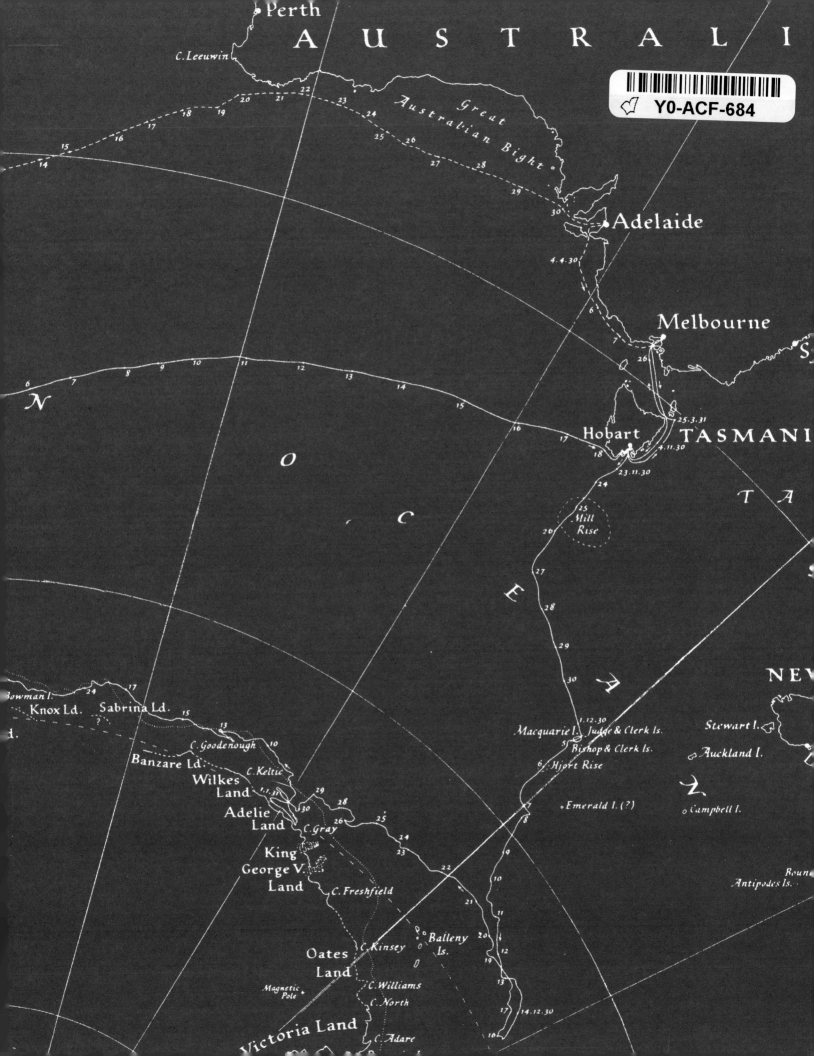

DOUGLAS MAWSON

The Life of an Explorer

DOUGLAS MAWSON

The Life of an Explorer

LINCOLN HALL

RESEARCH: BARBARA SCANLAN

NEW
HOLLAND

First published in Australia in 2000 by
New Holland Publishers (Australia) Pty Ltd
Sydney • Auckland • London • Cape Town

14 Aquatic Drive Frenchs Forest NSW 2086 Australia
218 Lake Road Northcote Auckland New Zealand
24 Nutford Place London W1H 6DQ United Kingdom
80 McKenzie Street Cape Town 8001 South Africa

Copyright © 2000 in text: Lincoln Hall
For details of copyright on all images, see page 221.

Created and produced by Lansdowne Publishing
Publisher: Deborah Nixon
Editor: Sarah Shrubb
Picture research: Barbara Scanlan
Designer: Mark Thacker, Big Cat Design
Project Co-ordinator: Clare Wallis

National Library of Australia Cataloguing-in-Publication Data:
Hall, Lincoln, 1955-.
  Douglas Mawson: the life of an explorer

        Bibliography.
        Includes index.
        ISBN 1 86436 670 2.

        1. Mawson, Douglas, Sir, 1882–1958. 2. Australasian Antarctic
        Expedition, (1911–1914). 3. Explorers - Australia - Biography.
        4. Antarctica - Discovery and exploration - Australia. I. Title.

        919.8904

The publishers would like to thank the above for their cooperation in providing pictures for use in this publication. Full effort has been made to locate the copyright owners of images and quotations within this book. We apologise for any omissions, which will be rectified in future editions.

For details of images on cover, title page and endpapers, see page 221.

Set in Garamond on QuarkXpress
Separated by Response Colour Graphics, Australia
Printed in Singapore by Tien Wah Press (Pte) Ltd

CONTENTS

INTRODUCTION

Douglas Mawson was very much a man of science. For him science was an adventure, but not the cerebral adventure of a quantum physicist, embroiled in a cycle of conjecture and nano-measurements in order to unveil the nature of the universe. Mawson's adventures were with a geology pick in his hand, revealing 600 million-year-old rocks, or exploring a horizon of limitless ice never before seen, let alone investigated. Mawson's excitement at being part of a rapidly changing world with areas still unmapped was passed onto the people he worked and explored with, and those he taught.

It was a sad day when I withdrew a 100-dollar note from the bank and saw that Sir Douglas Mawson's face was no longer looking at me intently with a hint of a smile. I had taken great satisfaction from his presence on our most valuable note, as I did with that of Sir Edmund Hillary on the New Zealand five-dollar bill. Millions of people had carried around in their pockets these endorsements from the makers of money and other powers-that-be, endorsements that adventure is worthwhile. Douglas Mawson, of course, is famous for exploring Antarctica, while Edmund Hillary's passion was for unclimbed mountains. I followed humbly in Hillary's footsteps, but like him, ultimately found myself pushing my limits beyond a southern horizon first mapped by Mawson.

Years ago in my first book about my role in the first Australian climb of Mt Everest, my aim was to show the human face of adventure. I addressed the same theme in my second book, the story of sailing as far south as anyone had ever sailed in a small yacht and then trudging inland from the Antarctic coast to climb a huge unclimbed mountain. On that expedition I re-acquainted myself with the terror of suddenly plummeting into a hidden crevasse, and for the first time I experienced the thankless toil of hauling an overloaded sledge behind me week after week. Tough as that was, I was no newcomer to hardship in extreme environments.

During my first Himalayan expedition ten years earlier I had lost toes to frostbite. On that climb, my friend and I were pushed to our limits as we battled to survive the descent from the mountaintop in a storm. Both of us sensed the 'presence' of a third person behind us, somehow guiding us. We didn't speak of this, or think anything of it in our desperate state, until we were safely in our tent below the danger zone. That experience has helped me to interpret in this book the 'presence' Douglas Mawson felt, which he refers to as Providence, when he battled for his life alone in the vast Antarctic wilderness. There are other connections, too, that my mountaineering experiences have allowed me to make.

Whether adventure is driven by the lure of a mountain peak or the lure of exploration, the differences in motivation vanish in survival situations because all thoughts and energies are directed to the most basic goal of staying alive. Adventure for science, for national glory, or for personal reasons, lead to the same insights and rewards, and the rewards can be great and unexpected in the sense of what you learn about yourself, about human nature and about reality.

The cultural context of the time provides the hook on which we peg our adventures, but I believe that the spirit of adventure which drives us to these places is the same throughout time. Some periods offered great opportunities for the most gripping of adventures, and one such period was the beginning of the 20th century

The days of Antarctic exploration are not yet over. Antarctica is commonly thought of as a vast plateau but it also has huge mountain ranges with many thousands of unclimbed peaks. During a voyage to the Antarctic Peninsula, we climbed this sub-peak from where we watched the glacial ice-cliffs opposite shed thousands of tonnes of ice into the bay. The photo shows the ice debris floating in an increasing circle. The following summer we made the first ascent of the mountain on the island in the background, Mt Don Roberts.

when Antarctica had been discovered in part but scarcely explored at all. Of course, achievements are due to the nature of the person and are not merely the product of the time and place they happen to find themselves in. Ernest Shackleton excelled as an adventurer and adjusted his integrity as was necessary to achieve his adventuring goals. Robert Falcon Scott's integrity was unassailable, but his approach to adventure was much more cautious and considered than Shackleton's. It is ironic that it was Scott who died, while Shackleton, taker of extraordinary risks, survived. Scott's position was further undermined by Roald Amundsen's superbly organised and efficiently run journey to the South Pole and back. Yet it is Scott who remains the great hero, perhaps because we can identity with his imperfections.

As for Douglas Mawson, his emphasis on science and exploration rather than the triumph of the human spirit did not spark the same worldwide enthusiasm achieved by Scott and Shackleton. The irony here is that Mawson demonstrated unequalled strength of spirit, but because he sought scientific knowledge and not a glory-soaked geographic symbol of adventure, he was overshadowed. Mawson was a prime mover in the 'heroic era' of Antarctic exploration, but unlike his contemporaries, his goals didn't include becoming a hero. Mawson unwittingly achieved heroic status but his ambition had been to feel the excitement of discovering unknown lands. He was not content with the simple mapping of coastlines but sought discovery in the full sense of exploring the nature of places which had never before been visited. Mere flag planting seemed a waste of time in his younger years, although as his career progressed, he came to appreciate that Australia's unique geographical relationship with Antarctica had relevance to Australia's significance as a nation.

Mawson's point of view needs to be seen in historical context. To understand his contribution to our knowledge of Antarctica, it is important to appreciate how scant that knowledge was when he first set foot on the frozen continent. At the beginning of the 20th century, Antarctica was the world's last great unknown, and there are good reasons why such a huge part of the Earth's surface remained a blank on the map at a time when all other continents had been explored, colonised and at least partly industrialised.

The existence of a great southern land had been first postulated by the Greeks in the sixth century B.C. but two thousand years passed before European nations had the knowledge and the means to undertake vast sea journeys to the furthest ends of the Earth. Navigators such as Diaz, Vasco da Gama, Magellan and Drake pushed the boundaries of the world known to Western civilisation, but it was not until 1771 that a British naval expedition set forth with the express purpose of determining whether or not the southern continent existed.

Commander of the voyage was James Cook, who only a few months earlier had returned from discovering the east coast of Australia, amongst other places. During his three-year voyage he circumnavigated Antarctica but the profusion of icebergs and pack ice rebuffed his every attempt to sight land. Cook was the first to cross the Antarctic Circle at 66° 33' South, and although he didn't discover land other than the South Sandwich Islands, he demonstrated that if Antarctica did exist, it undoubtedly lay in its entirety in an inhospitable frozen region. Cook's reports of huge numbers of whales and seals prompted whaling and sealing expeditions, some of which established temporary bases on sub-Antarctic islands, but the continent itself was not definitely sighted until 1831 by Captain John Briscoe. Pack-ice prevented Briscoe from landing on this section of coast, which lay due south from the tip of Africa.

During this period other important voyages took place which were to have ramifications for Douglas Mawson's travels in the next century. One of these was led by the French Admiral Durmont d'Urville, who reached the Antarctic mainland south of Australia in January, 1840. Once again pack ice prevented a landing on the continent, but Durmont d'Urville was able to land on an islet a few hundred metres off the coast, which he named Terre Adélie after his wife. D'Urville and his party toasted the occasion with a bottle of Bordeaux and claimed this section of coast for France. Another navigator who was to influence Mawson's plans was the American Charles Wilkes who also charted land south of Australia in the same year. Far more productive in terms of solid information about Antarctica were Sir James Clark Ross' summer voyages between 1839 and 1843, with winters spent in Australia and the Falkland Islands. Ross discovered land south of New Zealand. He named and landed on Possession Island, claimed the region for the British Crown, and named the mountainous coastline Victoria Land. He continued sailing south into a huge bay in the Antarctic coast, now known as the Ross Sea. This discovery opened the way for the most famous Antarctic expeditions of all, those with the goal of reaching the South Pole. Sixty-four years later it was this quest which provided Mawson with his ticket to Antarctica on an expedition which was to change the course of his life. Again it is a sign of the times that the explorers' focus, apart from Mawson's, was on reaching the South Pole rather than on determining the limits and the nature of the

A climber tackles a steep peak in the Everest region. The most extreme environment on Earth is found on the highest peaks of the Himalayas where jet-stream winds, extreme cold and the shortage of oxygen make a deadly combination. Yet even on Mt Everest, escape to the warmer oxygen-rich air is a mere few kilometres lower down, although reaching this comfort zone can take several days of careful down-climbing, more if trapped by a storm. In Antarctica there is no comfort zone. Temporary escape can be had in a hut or an ice-cave, but the bitter cold is always waiting outside.

continent, even though in the early 1900s it was not yet known whether Antarctica was a few giant islands joined by sea-ice or one immense continent.

The great Antarctic adventures are achievements of such magnitude and extreme hardship that the people who led them have gained mythic status. Mawson, Amundsen, Scott and Shackleton have been put on untouchable pedestals, yet these men are as human as the rest of us, who in their time had to deal with the same kinds of emotional, spiritual and mundane issues that all of us have to face. Their feats seem so extraordinary because their chosen arena is so foreign that it may as well be another planet. Even today, when Antarctic tourism has made the frozen continent more accessible than ever, the journeys of exploration in those technologically primitive times seem almost suicidal.

In my opinion, one of the reasons adventurers are questioned so intensively, particularly about motivation, is that they tend to display a zest for life which seems to contradict their willingness to face extreme danger. In the case of the great Antarctic explorers who are no longer here to field questions, books are written to analyse, explore or admire. Whether it is Scott, Mawson or Shackleton, book after book is written, stories are told and retold. That these books are still bought in their thousands shows that the fascination lingers, and that unanswered questions remain. Historians continue to unearth unpublished letters and misplaced diaries to support old theories or justify new ones. All this is an attempt to understand what made it possible for these men to achieve what they did, and the questions continue to be asked because adventure itself remains an enigma. Hopefully my perspective will help make the engines of adventure more understandable.

In this book, aided by previously unpublished photographs as well as those commonly seen, I hope to show the many sides of Douglas Mawson and hence demonstrate that despite his Antarctic feats, he was in many ways like the rest of us. In my research, as I read books, articles and reports, pored through photographs, talked to his family and other people who knew him, and admired the Mawson Antarctic Collection in Adelaide, I gained a sense of a man who had certainly been a great explorer and scientist, but also a man who had done 'normal' things such as falling in love, raising a family, planting trees, scolding the cat. His lesson to me is not to grab my ice-axe and head for the next unclimbed mountain, but to embrace the fabulous things that life has to offer — human companionship, the rewards of having a purpose, and the mysteries of the world.

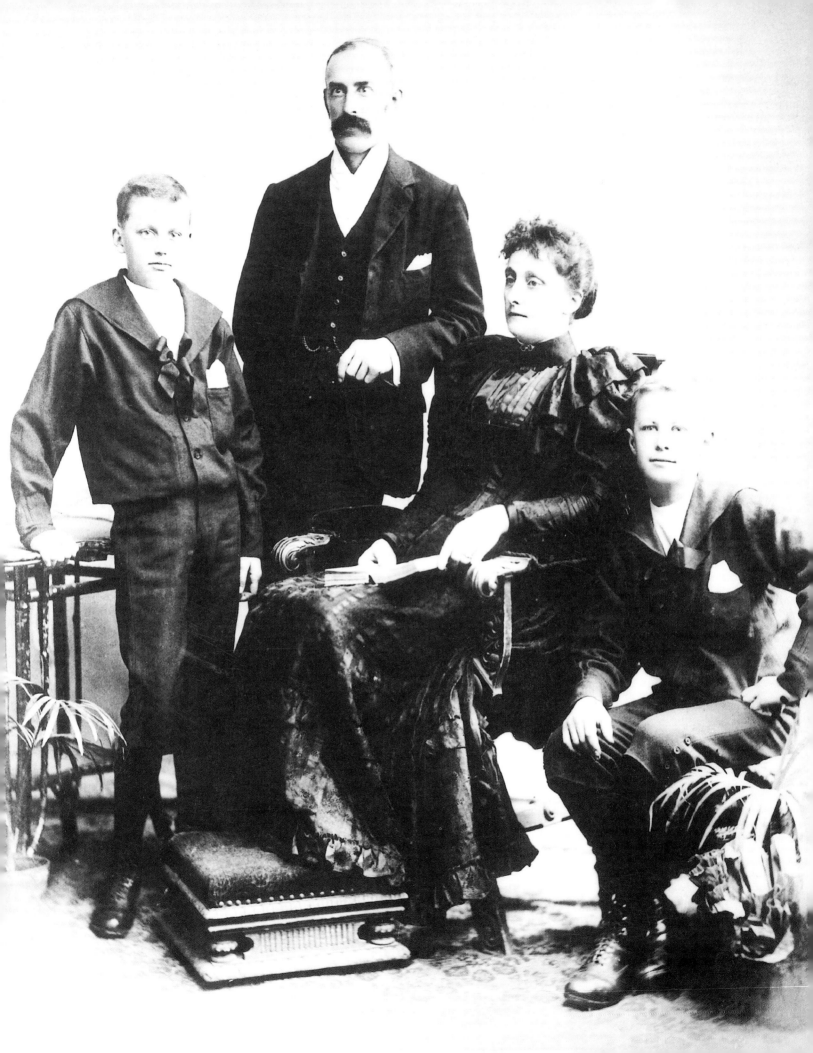

CHAPTER 1

The Young Mawson

The Mawson family in approximately 1892. Robert Ellis Mawson, at this time an accountant with a Sydney timber merchant, and his wife Margaret Ann, with their two sons, William, left, and Douglas, 10, who is already taller than his brother. Throughout their youth, Douglas was to keep abreast of his brother, who was two years older, even matriculating from Fort Street Model Public School in the same year, 1898.

Before he was three years old, Douglas Mawson found adventure at sea. On board the clipper *Ellora*, sailing from England to Australia, the toddler escaped from his cot, found his way onto the deck and immediately started climbing the rigging. He ignored all shouts from the deck and kept climbing up and up until a sailor clambered up the rigging after him and plucked the protesting youngster from the ropes. At the beginning of ***Mawson of the Antarctic***, Paquita Mawson's 1964 biography of her husband, Lady Mawson tells this tale of young Douglas. After describing the incident she leaves readers to draw their own conclusions. The inference is that Douglas Mawson was a born adventurer and risk-taker, who, if we were to indulge in clumsy symbolism, was destined for higher things. Of course, as every parent knows, children explore the world without fear until fear is instilled into them. But perhaps in Douglas' case the fear was less strongly inculcated than in many families, as his father, Robert Mawson was himself inspired by a sense of adventure.

Enticing as this idea may be, the truth is that little more than the bare facts are known about Douglas Mawson's childhood. He was born on 5 May 1882, on a farm

As a young man Douglas Mawson often went camping with his brother or university friends. He obviously felt comfortable in the bush, a handy attribute for a future geologist.

While studying for a Bachelor of Engineering at the University of Sydney, Mawson, second from left, was a founding member of the University Volunteer Rifle Corps, as was his mentor, T. W. Edgeworth David.

Mawson, left, with a friend by a campfire (recently fed for the photograph). Mawson's healthy respect for the elements from an early age proved to be valuable in Antarctica.

at Shipley, in the Wharfe Valley, near Bradford, Yorkshire. He was the second child of Robert and Margaret Mawson. Robert's forebears had farmed the valley for centuries, but this was not a tradition Robert Mawson aspired to carry on. Robert's own father had died when he was six, and when he was eight his mother sent him to a grammar school in York so that she could run the family farm. At school Robert acquired a love of learning and dreamed of exploring the South Seas. When his mother died – the year Douglas was born – Robert sold his interest in the farm and pursued his dream. There was adventure to be had exploring the South Seas but not the security desirable when raising a family. He compromised and decided to emigrate to Australia, then still seen as an outpost of the British Empire. It was a place with prospects for proper schooling and, Robert Mawson hoped, entrepreneurial opportunities. And so it was that in 1884 the Mawsons set sail for Australia – Robert, Margaret, two-year-old Douglas and four-year-old William – on a ten-week voyage to Sydney.

Although Robert had travelled to the other side of the world to avoid the family tradition of farming, the Mawsons settled on a farm near Rooty Hill, in what is now Sydney's western suburbs. However, Australian farming was very different, particularly the Robert Mawson way. His experiments with the new technology of fruit-canning were not a success, so eventually he sold the farm and took a job as the accountant for a timberyard in Sydney. The family moved to Glebe, and in 1895 Douglas enrolled in Fort Street Model Public School, an institution responsible for educating many prominent Australians. Douglas was a very good student, capable and with an interest in his studies. This combination allowed him to complete his schooling early. In 1898 Headmaster J.W. Turner is believed to have made some extraordinary farewell remarks about him: 'What shall we say of our Douglas as an acknowledged leader and organiser? This I will say: that if there be a corner of this planet of ours still unexplored, Douglas Mawson will be the organiser and leader of an expedition to unveil its secrets.'

These remarks at his final school speech night were remarkably prophetic. Perhaps at age 16 Mawson echoed in some ways his father's ambitions of exploration, although his father exhibited these in a way unlikely to be approved of by Headmaster Turner.

As the boys were finishing their schooling, Robert Mawson headed off to New Guinea, where he intended to make his fortune. Robert excused himself to his wife, saying he was sure the boys would win scholarships to university, which they did, but they were arts scholarships and neither wanted to study arts. William wanted to study medicine and Douglas mining engineering. Their mother encouraged them to follow their desires, which were far more practical than her husband's, and she made the money to put them through university by turning their Glebe home into a boarding house.

In March 1899, still aged 16 but tall for his age, Douglas enrolled at the University of Sydney. At the turn of the century mining engineering promised him a career with unlimited potential. His enthusiasm was noticed by T. W. Edgeworth David, Professor of Geology, who channelled some of Mawson's youthful energy into some of his own projects, such as the sinking of an exploratory shaft into the coal seams near Maitland in the Hunter Valley. Edgeworth David had established his considerable repu-tation by mapping the entire system of coal seams in the Greta region and adjacent parts

T. W. Edgeworth David, Professor of Geology at the University of Sydney from 1891 to 1924, inspired Mawson to change the direction of his career from mining engineering to geology.

of the Hunter Valley. The great economic importance of these coal fields led to Edgeworth David gaining not only the respect of his peers but a position of influence with government. He was helped in all of these endeavours, as well as in his teaching, by his charm, enthusiasm and good humour. Edgeworth David was popular with his students, and although the Professor did not like having favourites, he could not help but respond to Mawson's talent and passion for geology. Their relationship, which evolved from its starting point of student and mentor to one of equals, was to be lifelong.

In 1902, Mawson completed his degree in mining engineering and immediately applied for a job as a junior chemistry demonstrator, so that he could help pay his

In 1902 Mawson worked as a junior chemistry demonstrator at the University of Sydney to help finance his second degree, a Bachelor of Science majoring in geology.

way through his second degree, this time in geology. He got the job, but at the suggestion of Edgeworth David it was on the condition that he was allowed six months' leave in April 1903 to join an expedition to the New Hebrides (now Vanuatu). This was no junket holiday disguised as a field trip. He left Sydney on the *Ysabel*, under the command of Captain Ernest Rason, a seasoned British Navy officer who was Deputy Commissioner of the New Hebrides. Mawson learnt that while he and biologist W.T. Quaife conducted their scientific studies, Rason would attend to unrest among the New Hebrideans. It promised to be an exciting time.

While Mawson was a passenger on *Ysabel*, Ernest Shackleton was also sailing north, returning to England from Antarctica. It was to be several years yet before Mawson met Shackleton, but it would be an important meeting for both men. Sub-lieutenant Shackleton was returning from Robert Falcon Scott's first expedition to Antarctica, invalided home after contracting scurvy while making the first-ever attempt to reach the South Pole with Scott and Edward Wilson. They had used dogs to pull their sleds to 82°16' South, further south than anyone had been but still 800 kilometres short of the Pole. They had pushed themselves almost too far, and had resorted to eating some of their sledge dogs as they struggled back to their base at Ross Island. Shackleton was the worst affected by scurvy and Scott insisted that he return to England on board the supply ship *Morning*. On the long voyage north Shackleton had time to make his own plans. Back in England, 60 years after Britain's last Antarctic expedition — by Sir James Clark Ross — Shackleton was greeted enthusiastically. He later attempted to turn this enthusiasm into funds for his own expedition, which also had the declared intention of reaching the South Pole.

By the time Shackleton was being lauded in London, Mawson had also reached his destination. The ship docked at Port Vila on 13 April, and Mawson was able to begin his geological survey on the spot, starting with the harbour, then moving up through the inland to include the entire island of Efate. This project took five weeks. Next was a voyage on Ernest Rason's ship HMS *Archer*, under the command of Captain Rolleston, north-west to the island of Malekula, the second-largest island and the home of cannibals. Only a partial survey was possible.

Further to the north-west was Santo, the largest island in the group. Here Mawson selected the summit of Mt Losumbunu as one of his survey points, a peak that no European had climbed. With the help of three islanders, Mawson and Quaife set out for Losumbunu, but they were turned back by the dense tropical jungle, swirling mist and, on a second attempt, lack of enthusiasm on the part of their guides. Mawson managed to climb to within 400 metres of the summit. It is arguable that from a geological point of view his time would have have been better spent concentrating on the more accessible points of this island, which until his arrival was

During his six-month geological survey of the New Hebrides (Vanuatu), 21-year-old Mawson took a number of fine quality large format photographs, including this village scene.

While his sons were in the last year of school, Robert Mawson set out to fulfil his original dream of adventure and prosperity in the South Seas, but only managed to make a passable living as copra merchant. Here he sits on the verandah of 'The Palace', his home in New Guinea.

Mawson brought back a number of artefacts from the New Hebrides, including this carved spoon and digging adze with a shell as a blade. Both have Mawson's hand-written labels.

completely unmapped geologically. It is a good example of Mawson directing both his love of science and his sense of adventure to a very physically demanding goal, and one beyond the call of duty. With this approach, great things could be achieved.

On his expedition to the New Hebrides Mawson lived the exotic life that his father had long dreamed about and had recently tried to make a reality. Robert Mawson went to New Guinea under the guise of making his fortune from the untapped resources of this unknown land, but in truth he sought adventure for its own sake. This was very different to the approach taken by his son, who explored under the banner of science with the appropriate training in a field with enormous economic potential. Mawson was inspired by the marvels of the natural world but he was also pragmatic.

On a professional level, his New Hebridean sojourn gave Mawson the opportunity to produce an 80-page report which was published in the ***Proceedings of the Linnean Society of New South Wales***. It was one of the first detailed geological reports of a group of South Pacific islands. This was a notable achievement for a new graduate, but a not exceptional one in those times. One hundred years ago there were many gaps in basic scientific knowledge. In many disciplines fundamental data had yet to be gathered from the less populated, un-Westernised parts of the world. But it was important work, as from the straightforward gathering of data simple conclusions could be drawn, and more advanced research could be planned.

Mawson returned to his job as chemistry tutor at the University of Sydney, and completed his studies in 1904, graduating with his Bachelor of Science degree in geology in 1905. He had already decided that for the time being at least his future lay in the academic world rather than in business, so he applied for the position of lecturer in mineralogy and petrology at the University of Adelaide. He was given the job and took up the position in March 1905.

Mawson was keen to explore the different geological landscapes within striking distance of Adelaide. In 1906 he began his first studies of the geology of the Broken

One of the few surviving informal photos showing Mawson as a strikingly handsome young man is this one of him sitting with a woman named Eileen Brougham.

Hill district, across the border in New South Wales. Here he was able to apply his knowledge of radioactivity, a subject he'd taken a particular interest in as a student, by identifying Australia's first substantial deposit of uranium ore, at what later became Radium Hill. He named the mineral davidite in honour of his mentor. His geological studies in the Broken Hill region were to gain him his Doctor of Science degree in 1909.

During university holidays Mawson took the opportunity to travel. His was not just the common youthful interest in new horizons; he was interested in the geological composition of those horizons and how they related to nearby horizons he had visited. In January 1907 his explorations took him to the summit of

Mt Kosciuszko with Griffith Taylor, fellow geologist and friend from student days at Sydney, his brother William, now a qualified and practising doctor, and W.T. Quaife, from the New Hebrides expedition. A trip to the Snowy Mountains was quite an undertaking in those days, and it was the first time Mawson saw a landscape shaped by glaciers, a subject which was to become of great interest to him in the very near future.

Unbeknownst to Mawson, Edgeworth David had written to Shackleton, requesting a position on his upcoming British Antarctic Expedition (B.A.E.). Edgeworth David, who was almost 50, stated that he was interested only in travelling to the Ross Sea and back on the expedition vessel, not in wintering-over. Shackleton had managed to raise most of the money he needed for his own attempt to reach to the South Pole and he was in the throes of choosing his expedition staff and ship's crew from over 400 applicants. He had bought *Nimrod*, a old sealing vessel, and refitted it for the voyage south. But he was still well short of his budget and, having exhausted sponsorship possibilities in Britain, he decided to set sail for southern waters and raise the necessary funds in Australia and New Zealand. To this end, he added Edgeworth David to the expedition list. Shackleton saw the fundraising opportunities of having his science program conducted in part by a prominent Australian who had influence with the government. Edgeworth David was delighted. When Mawson became aware of the expedition and of Edgeworth David's presence on it, he wrote to his old professor that: 'I should dearly have loved to have gone myself.'

As a young man, Mawson was enthusiastic about his geology, taking every opportunity to join field trips or go bush by himself, sometimes on his bicycle.

Edgeworth David inspired Mawson to take up geology, but perhaps his love of rocks throughout his life stemmed from his talent for identifying the geological processes which formed them. Here are a few of the many thousands of specimens he collected.

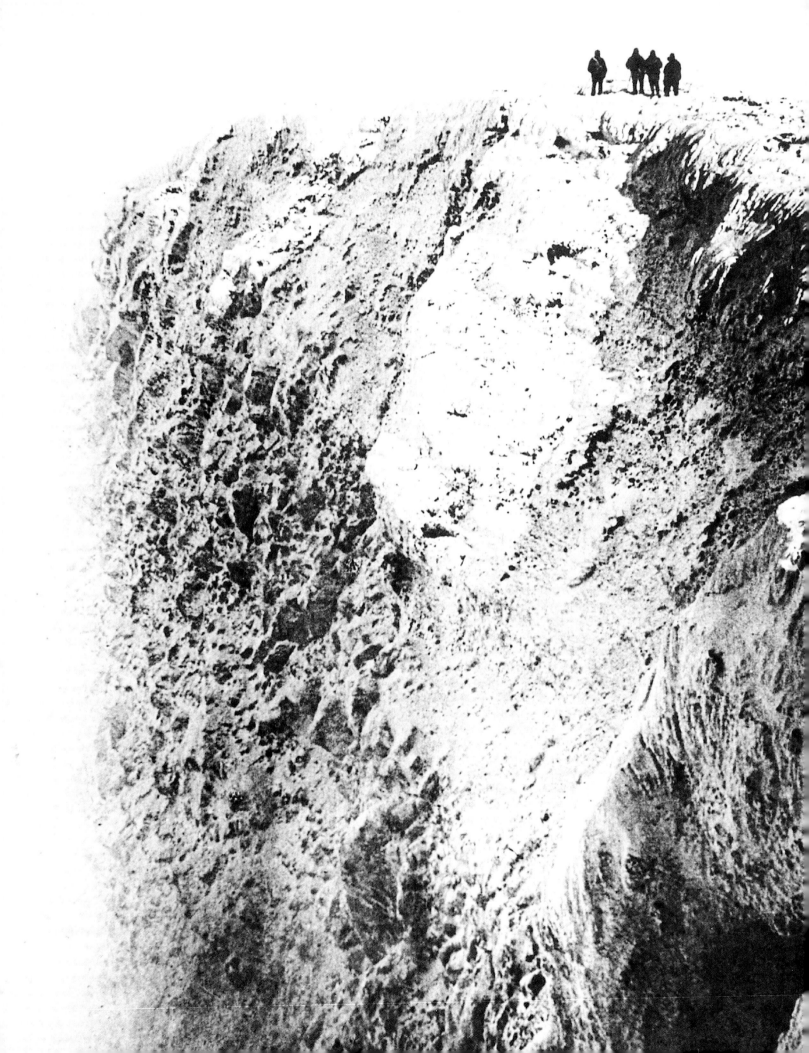

CHAPTER 2

The Shackleton School

*After surviving a 30-hour blizzard without tents,
sheltering only in their three-man sleeping bags,
five of the six climbers reached the summit
crater to see the amazing contrast of steam
hissing from the depths while they stood in
sub-zero temperatures.*

Given the position of the natural sciences in the early years of the century, it is easy to understand why academia appealed to Douglas Mawson. As a new graduate he had been able to contribute to the growing understanding of the geology of the Western Pacific region, and he'd had fun in the process. In Australia, everywhere Mawson looked there was a wealth of geological exploration to be done. The key was to make the most of his opportunities. With a little self-help, Edgeworth David had found an opportunity to go to Antarctica, a continent about which less was known than any other place on Earth. The idea excited Mawson, and what was good for the mentor sounded good to the protégé.

When Shackleton passed through Adelaide on his journey from Britain to Sydney, Mawson took the opportunity to introduce himself and offer his services as a geologist at no cost to the expedition, stating that he hoped to witness glaciers in the process of weathering mountain ranges, knowledge which would help him interpret the 600-million year-old glacial sediments that he was studying in South Australia. A few days later Shackleton telegraphed Mawson that he would like to appoint him Expedition Physicist, not just for the following year's summer, which had been Mawson's suggestion, but for the duration of the 15-month expedition, and with a stipend of £200 per annum. Mawson was certainly surprised, partly because he was a geologist not a physicist, but he accepted the position because he considered it too good an opportunity to miss. Antarctica had captured both public and scientific imagination, and it is possible that Mawson realised joining the expedition – even as 'route surveyor, cartographer, and magnetician', which were to be his main duties – was a smart career move. One factor that influenced his decision to accept Shackleton's offer was that Edgeworth David had chosen to travel south only for the first summer; after Edgeworth David's departure Mawson felt sure that his own role could be expanded to include geology.

Mawson had joined an expedition that was poised to capitalise on the achievements of the team led by Scott in 1901–04. Shackleton presented lectures about Antarctica in Sydney and Melbourne. Many tickets were sold and his talks were very well received. As part of his fundraising strategy he invested the proceeds from his lectures by donating them to charities. As intended, this act made a favourable impression and helped create the feeling that his expedition was a magnanimous one, destined to bring glory to the British Empire. With the help of friendly words

Shackleton, always aware of the value of appearances, allowed the expedition ship Nimrod *to be gloriously farewelled by a crowd of 30,000 as it steamed out of Lyttelton Harbour, New Zealand. Away from the crowds, it was attached by towline to Koonya, and towed south to the Antarctic Circle, a tactic used to compensate for choosing an expedition ship that was too small to carry both the expedition supplies and sufficient coal to get to Antarctica.*

from Edgeworth David in the ear of Prime Minister Alfred Deakin, the Australian government gave Shackleton a much-needed grant of £5000. Putting together such a lengthy expedition was a logistical nightmare, but Shackleton had taken care of many of these details before leaving Britain. Nevertheless, Mawson had a busy two-and-a-half months from the time he was invited to join the British Antarctic Expedition until December 1907, when he sailed from Sydney to join the ship at Lyttelton, the port of Christchurch, New Zealand.

Mawson's first diary entry of the journey on 20 December 1907, during the five-day voyage by passenger liner from Sydney to New Zealand, records the natural interests of a young man setting forth on a long, all-male expedition to a bleak uninhabited land. He wrote: 'The Blue Moon Dramatic Company, 75 of them, were fellow passengers to Wellington...as mal-de-mer wore off, they made the most of the opportunity to show what wondrous fellow feeling there is between the sexes. At this stage things might be well described as red hot, even at midnight on the main deck.' Mawson had the height, build and looks to cope with such a situation.

Conditions on board the SY *Nimrod*, the vessel Shackleton had purchased for the voyage south to Antarctica, were far less appealing, but the group was given a magnificent send off from Christchurch's Lyttelton Harbour on Regatta Day, at the beginning of the New Year, 1908. Their ship was towed by SS *Koonya* in order to save coal. Nimrod was overloaded, and the quarters for the expeditioners were extremely cramped and uncomfortable. Mawson was among the many who were seasick, and he took to sleeping in a lifeboat, where vomiting was less of a nuisance to his companions. He was found in this state by John King Davis, First Officer of *Nimrod*, who brought him some tinned pears to eat. Twelve hours later Davis brought more pears, and seeing that Mawson looked better, he convinced him to go below for hot cocoa. This was the beginning of a lifelong friendship but one that was to be tested often, sometimes in dangerous circumstances, by Mawson's single-mindedness and Davis' fiery temper.

Meanwhile, Edgeworth David was busy writing two letters to be sent back with *Koonya*. The first was to the University of Sydney, advising that rather than making the three-month round trip initially arranged, he intended to stay with the expedition for its 15-month duration. The second letter was a similar message to his wife. When Shackleton first met Edgeworth David, he had been much taken by the distinguished man's presence, charm and maturity – the very qualities needed to maintain morale among the men – and he convinced Edgeworth David that life would be better for them both if he joined the expedition for its duration. David felt that the only sure way to be granted leave by both the university and his wife was to present his absence as *fait accompli*.

The ships passed their first iceberg on 24 January, and the following day the sky above the horizon held the white tinge of 'ice-blink', the reflection of pack-ice. *Koonya* turned to the north, having claimed to have established a record as the first steel-hulled vessel to have crossed the Antarctic Circle and towed the expedition vessel for over 4200 kilometres. *Nimrod* now fended for itself under the captaincy of Lieutenant Rupert England. Shackleton had planned to establish his base towards the eastern limits of the Great Ice Barrier which spanned the 1000-kilometre width of the Ross Sea, but he was startled to see that the icescape was now dramatically different from the one he had seen from Scott's ship *Discovery* five years earlier. He feared that the ice was unstable, so he instructed England to sail to the west along the icecoast to Ross Island, which was permanently frozen into the ice of the Barrier.

The B.A.E. landed at Cape Royds, 30 kilometres north of Scott's old base. On 3 February the team began to unload their supplies for the upcoming year, and shortly afterwards *Nimrod* steamed away to the north, its next visit a full year away. The following weeks were spent assembling the small expedition hut and organising it as efficiently as possible to accommodate 15 men through the long, dark winter. Of these 15, only Shackleton, Frank Wild and Ernest Joyce had previous polar experience, all three having participated in Scott's *Discovery* expedition. Shackleton, of course, was in charge of the expedition, Wild was in charge of stores and Joyce's chief responsibility was the sled dogs. The expedition was heavily weighted with geologists – 21-year-old Raymond Priestley was engaged for the job in Britain by Shackleton, and he assigned the position of assistant geologist to Sir Philip Brocklehurst, a young man from a wealthy family who paid handsomely for his passage. W.T. Edgeworth David at age 50 was the most accomplished geologist, and although Mawson was engaged as a physicist, Shackleton also commissioned him to do geological and survey work. The rest of the team consisted of two doctors, Eric Marshall and Alistair Mackay, James Murray as biologist, Jameson Adams as meteorologist, and William Roberts as cook. Bertram Armytage, an Australian cavalry soldier who had been based in Britain, was in charge of the expedition's ponies. Bernard Day was a mechanic and George Marston an artist, but both also worked as handymen. Joyce had learnt taxidermy specifically so that the expedition could bring back specimens of wildlife, and he and Wild took a crash course in typesetting in London so they could fulfil Shackleton's ambition of printing Antarctica's first book. That was a job planned for the long, dark winter, but at the beginning of March the days still held enough daylight for exploration to be done.

Although Scott's expedition had been based here between 1902 and 1904, an obvious challenge with obvious scientific interest remained untouched. This was the ascent of Mt Erebus, a huge active volcano whose slopes began at the back of their hut. At 3794 metres it was the highest point of Ross Island. When Edgeworth David suggested that a party attempt to climb Mt Erebus, Shackleton appointed him leader of the climb, with Mawson and Mackay as the other members of the summit team. Foreseeing the difficulty of climbing steep ice, they equipped themselves with home-made crampons – spiked metal frames which are strapped to the underside of boots.

Shackleton had hoped to set up the expedition base on the ice at the Bay of Whales, but conditions had changed dramatically since his visit with Scott in 1902, making him think it was too risky to spend the winter on what was obviously unstable ice. Instead he sailed west to Ross Island, an area of much greater interest to the geologists Edgeworth David and Douglas Mawson. This had been Scott's base for their foray towards the Pole. Before leaving England Shackleton had promised Scott he would explore a different route from a different base, but he now felt that the might of Nature, rather than a gentleman's word, was calling the shots.

Their homemade versions were metal spikes riveted to a leather sole which was then strapped to the underside of a boot. Adams, Brocklehurst and Marshall formed the support party to help haul the sledge.

On 5 March, the six men set off on what was very much a journey of discovery for all of them, not only because Erebus was unclimbed, but also because this was to be their first experience of extended travel in Antarctica. On the first day they easily avoided crevassed glaciers but had to lift their sledge over low rocky ridges of moraine. They also made the acquaintance of 'sastrugi', ridges of ice between 10 centimetres and two metres high caused by wind erosion, which are the curse of all polar sledging parties, even today. The team covered a distance of 11 kilometres and climbed to an altitude of 840 metres. That evening they set up their two tents and cooked up their first 'hoosh'. Although polar exploration was only in its infancy, hoosh was already legendary fare. It consisted of pemmican (dried tinned beef and fruit) boiled up with fragments of biscuits or whatever other food scraps were available.

The next day they crawled out of their three-man, reindeer skin sleeping bags into temperatures of -23°C. Steeper ground and more sastrugi awaited them, making their climb of five kilometres up to 1700 metres hard work, especially for those in the support party who had not made themselves crampons. This difficult terrain led to the decision to leave the sledge behind. The whole party of six elected to push on, carrying all that they needed on their backs. They cached the sledge, tent floors and poles, food for the return journey and some of their cooking utensils, then pushed on up the mountain with sleeping bags, survey equipment and three days' rations, carrying these by whatever means they could improvise. Mawson was also carrying a heavy plate camera, as photography was one of his duties. They were slowed down by the steep and unforgiving slopes of the huge summit cone, but were able to find a recess in a rocky ridge large enough for them to make their camp. This bedding down was achieved quickly, as all they had to do after cooking up their hoosh was crawl inside their sleeping bags and drape the pole-less tents over the entrance to keep out windblown snow. By the morning a blizzard was in progress, and the men had no choice but to spend the day lying in their bags. The blizzard continued to rage through the night. Lighting the kerosene stove to melt snow for drinks was out of the question, but they were able munch on biscuits and chocolate.

By the next morning the somewhat daunted expeditioners were able to continue – up the steepest part of the climb. The route posed no particular mountaineering

difficulties but the men roped themselves together to protect those members who did not have crampons. They followed rocky ridges where they could, then Mackay untied from the rope at one point and with his ice-axe chopped a line of steps directly up the final steep slope. He underestimated the effort involved and fainted. After Edgeworth David and Marshall revived him, the party hurried along the rim until they found a campsite. Brocklehurst's feet were frostbitten, so he spent the next day in one of the sleeping bags while the others climbed up to the main crater. Mawson was kept particularly busy in his attempts to take photos, as the focal plane of the camera had become frozen.

When at last they crested the rim of the active crater, the spectacular sight was worth the hardship and the effort they had endured. Steam clouds filled the sheer-walled 800-metre wide crater and swirled upwards for hundreds of metres. Booms and hisses signalled the volcanic activity hidden in the steam. There was enough of a clearing for Mawson to measure the depth of the crater – around 270 metres – while Marshall made measurements to determine the altitude of the summit. The estimated height was 4075 metres, 280 metres above that determined decades later by modern surveying techniques. They hurried down from the summit as they were keen to get frostbitten Brocklehurst down the steep slopes of the main crater that day. They arrived back at the hut at Cape Royds to an enthusiastic welcome.

The climb of Erebus was a great adventure, but was certainly no model of how such an excursion should be undertaken. Crampons were manufactured during the last hours before departure and not all members had them, which was a ludicrous situation when attempting the first-ever climb of a major Antarctic mountain. Their depot of equipment and food halfway up the volcano had been blown in all directions by a blizzard; Marshall found the quarter-plate camera in a snow drift but many things were lost altogether. Because of their long bamboo poles, their tents were not suitable for carrying unless strapped to a sledge, and yet the team chose a route which was only sledgable to less than halfway up the mountain. (Sledges were later hauled to a camp 1000 metres higher by the second ascent party in 1912 during Scott's expedition.) The chances of surviving a blizzard are severely reduced without a tent, an outcome Edgeworth David's team no doubt pondered when trapped in their sleeping bags for 30 hours. On the descent they were lucky to escape serious injury when they slid down the steepest snow and ice slopes. They also lost and damaged more equipment by rolling their loads in bags down the snow slopes.

Unfamiliarity with the realities of Antarctica was one reason for these errors, but incomplete planning and confusion in decision-making were others. Shackleton had appointed Adams in charge of the overall exercise but he put Edgeworth David in charge of the climb. When both the support and the ascent team pushed for the top this system fell apart, at a time when they were high on the first real mountain any of them had climbed in an inhospitable continent none of them knew very much about. This might seem to us like a slapdash approach, but it was how the parameters of Antarctic exploration were determined in what was aptly called the 'Heroic Era'.

From the point of view of the British Antarctic Expedition, all was well that ended well, particularly when valuable lessons were learnt. The success of the climb carried the whole expedition into winter with high morale. Already they had a major achievement under their belts, and the severity of the conditions left no-one with any delusions about what to expect on the longer journeys scheduled for the spring and summer.

By the end of March the days were getting noticeably shorter. Everyone was busy with projects around the base. Mawson determined the nature of the different deposits of snow and ice as well as rock, and assisted Jameson Adams with his meteorological work.

Shackleton was very aware of the need to keep his men occupied in the cramped quarters of the hut during winter, and it was to this end that he had brought a small printing press and most of the resources necessary to produce a book. One thing still lacking was material for book covers, so Bernard Day improvised these out of packing cases. The men contributed to the project in different ways. Edgeworth David wrote an account of the ascent of Mt Erebus while Mawson submitted 'Bathybia', a fantasy about a lush, hidden Antarctic world at the mysterious South Pole inhabited by giant spiders and exploding mushrooms.

The expedition hut measured 10 metres long by 5.8 metres wide by 2.4 metres high, which was very small given that it had to accommodate not only 15 men and an enormous amount of equipment, but also a photographic dark room, printing press, kitchen, and work area for writing reports and making or modifying equipment. Mawson shared a two-bunk alcove with Edgeworth David – it was always so cluttered with scientific equipment that other expeditioners called it the Pawn Shop. The team was a mix of strong personalities from varied backgrounds, but when tensions arose they were usually diffused by Edgeworth David's charm or

Shackleton's subtle manipulations. However, on one occasion Mackay attacked Roberts, the cook, and Mawson had to prise Mackay's hands away from Roberts' neck. Luckily this was in August, when the promise of escape from the interminable darkness and the confines of the hut was near.

During the winter, plans for the major sledging journeys of the spring and summer had been refined. Paramount in Shackleton's eyes was the journey to the South Pole, which he would undertake with Frank Wild, Eric Marshall and Jameson Adams. Never afraid of setting himself tough goals, Shackleton wanted his expedition to be doubly victorious by being the first to reach both the South Geographic Pole, the world's most southerly point, and the South Magnetic Pole, which lay approximately 650 kilometres north-north-west of Ross Island. He put Edgeworth David in charge of this northbound team and David later assigned Douglas Mawson and Alistair Forbes Mackay to accompany him.

In August, still in darkness, Shackleton led Armytage and Edgeworth David on a reconnaissance to Scott's old base at Hut Point, 30 kilometres to the south. Then began the relaying of supplies for the push to the South Pole, with all novices getting a taste of sledging as Shackleton laid his furthest depot, 160 kilometres to the south.

Shackleton had equipped the expedition with many gadgets then at the cutting edge of technology. Among these was an Arrol-Johnston motor car, which he hoped would be useful in hauling supplies across the level terrain of the sea-ice. On 22 September they drove across 12 kilometres of ice, to the limits of the wind-packed snow cover. After this Shackleton made the car available to the Magnetic Pole party. Mawson was sceptical about its efficiency as a load hauler, and left others to experiment while he busied himself with other preparations. Two depots were established, 16 kilometres and 24 kilometres from base, before Edgeworth David, Mackay and Priestley decided that the effort and hardship of using the car was more trouble than it was worth. While struggling with the car Mackay suffered a fractured bone in his wrist, so he began the sledge journey with his arm in a sling.

On 5 October, a week before Shackleton headed south, Edgeworth David, Mawson and Mackay began their journey to the north. When they left the hut at Cape Royds, Edgeworth David was 50 years old, Alistair Forbes Mackay was 30 and Douglas Mawson was 26. Despite Mawson being the youngest, Shackleton had instructed him to take charge should anything happen to Edgeworth David. Their main goal was set as the South Magnetic Pole, but Shackleton was also keen for

Mawson and Edgeworth David were indeed thrown in the Antarctic deep end with their ascent of Mt Erebus, the active volcano which is the most obvious feature of Ross Island. It was the first-ever ascent of a major Antarctic peak, undertaken by a team of six, all of whom were novices to mountaineering. The expedition base is visible in the middle foreground.

them to prospect for economic minerals in the enigmatic Dry Valley, a snow-free area to the west of Ross Island that had been discovered by Scott in 1901. He also asked them to make a geological survey of the coast of Victoria Land. It was a grand plan indeed, and it quickly became apparent that it was an overambitious one for three men without dogs, ponies or a support crew! However, the team was instructed that if they were delayed, they were to head for the coast. By this time *Nimrod* would have returned to Antarctica from New Zealand, and when they saw the ship which would be sent north from Ross Island in search of them, they were to signal it with a heliograph (mirror).

The small team headed out across the sea-ice, making slow progress because they had to relay their loads. On 13 October they reached the Antarctic mainland at Butter Point, virtually due west of Cape Royds. From there they headed north, following the coastline but remaining on the sea-ice.

At the beginning of the South Magnetic Pole journey Mawson took up writing in his diary, a discipline he hadn't followed since the expedition arrived at Cape Royds. His diary gives a valuable insight into what was the most important part of the expedition, from Mawson's point of view. Mawson's propensity for achieving a goal by breaking it down into achievable, monitorable sections became apparent as their trek progressed. On 22 October, as navigator he announced that their several goals were unachievable, given the projected distance to the South Magnetic Pole. He suggested they fulfil two of Shackleton's three directives, namely the mapping and geological surveys of the Victoria Land coast and Dry Valley. Mawson was interested in the exciting discoveries to be made along an entire coastline which had not been more than sketch-mapped from a distance, and in the enigmatic, snowless Dry Valley. These were goldmines for the keen young geologist, far more worthwhile than the probably unachievable trudge to the spot where the dip circle compass needle would point down vertically to the South Magnetic Pole. Reaching the 'Mag Pole', as he called it, would be a milestone, but it would do little to increase scientific understanding of Antarctica.

However, Edgeworth David was adamant that their primary goal would remain the Magnetic Pole, and that they must complete as much geological and survey work as could be managed while they travelled. He was a renowned geologist at the peak of his career, and he saw value in chasing the milestone. Mackay, too, was lured by the romance of this goal. Although he was overridden by Edgeworth David's

On the ascent of Mt Erebus all members of the party had their first experience of sledge hauling, although on the route they adopted the slope soon became too steep and all equipment and provisions had to be carried in improvised knapsacks.

authority (with Mackay's vote thrown in), Mawson had made an important point, which was that for any hope of success they must increase the distance covered each day from their average of six kilometres. This was a difficult proposition as they were still travelling by relay. The three men would haul one sledge, then go back and haul the other, which meant every kilometre gained by the sledges involved them travelling three kilometres by foot.

A week passed, during which time Mawson had adequate time to ponder their predicament. In his diary for 29 October he wrote, 'I cannot see how it is at all possible for us to reach the Magnetic Pole in one season under such conditions', but by that evening he had come up with a game plan. He suggested that they forget about their other objectives, save full rations for the estimated 700-kilometre return journey inland from the coast, and meanwhile 'live on seal flesh and local food cooked by local means as much as possible'. He also added that when they returned to the coast after the inland journey the frozen sea-ice would have broken up into pack-ice and they would be committed to waiting there at their depot for *Nimrod* to cruise by, as arranged. Both Edgeworth David and Mackay accepted his proposal and its implications. They added seals and penguins to their diet and Mackay fashioned a cooker which used seal blubber as its fuel.

Now that they were heading north along the coast they took advantage of the southerly winds by rigging sails on their sledges. They also adopted the tactic of travelling at night, when the few extra degrees of frost made the soft surface snow firmer. Daytime air temperatures were usually around 6°C, but when the sun was shining the surface of the snow sometimes rose above freezing point, making for much heavier going. Another factor which worked against them was the combined effect of the damp sea air and the saline content of the snow, making the surface snow sticky and less compacted. In an attempt to increase progress they cached food and geological specimens and some food on an islet they named Depot Island. It was over a month before they realised how much the sea-ice conditions limited their progress; on 11 November they reached the Nordenskjöld Ice Tongue, where glacial ice pushed though a gap in the Prince Albert Mountains and flowed out into the Ross Sea as a peninsula of freshwater ice. Travel was much easier on the surface of the glacial tongue than on the sea-ice, and the 50-metre rise gave Mawson the opportunity to measure the angles and directions to several prominent mountains. The northern side of the ice tongue was steep and difficult to descend so the sledges had to be unloaded and supplies lowered by rope.

The 12–15 horsepower New Arrol-Johnston motorcar, fitted with a specially designed air-cooled four-cylinder engine, had been brought from Scotland by Shackleton. It was used to establish two depots for the South Magnetic Pole party on the sea-ice between Ross Island and the west coast of the Ross Sea. However, it proved to be frustratingly temperamental in the cold, which is not surprising, given the basic nature of automobile engineering in 1907. Inappropriate wheels made the car virtually useless if soft snow covered the surface to a depth of any more than a few centimetres.

For another month they followed the coast north, looking for a way through to what they expected to be an ice plateau beyond the coastal mountains. Two weeks of this month were spent crossing the 30-kilometre wide Drygalski Barrier Tongue, with its complicated terrain of ice ridges and crevasses. When they reached the far side of the Drygalski they established a depot, deciding it was time to forge a way inland up one of the several glaciers cutting through the Prince Albert Mountains. They left one of their two sledges behind, as well as some equipment and a small amount of food, and marked the depot with a flag. They also left letters outlining their intentions, signing off to their families in case they did not return.

At this point it's worth considering the loneliness of their situation. For 10 weeks they had been travelling across the sea-ice and glacial tongues, where the terrain sometimes dictated a very circuitous route. While they remained on the coast they could take solace in Shackleton's emergency plan: they could be picked up anywhere along the coast south of Cape Washington by *Nimrod* after the ship had returned to Cape Royds. But once they commenced the journey inland they would be utterly on their own until they returned to the shores of the Ross Sea. Had they been starting fresh from their base, rather than from the coast, the prospect of a

While Mawson was preparing to journey in search of the South Magnetic Pole with Edgeworth David and Forbes Mackay, Shackleton and his three companions had already left on their push towards the South Geographic Pole, with Manchurian ponies to pull their sledges and a support party hauling extra supplies. None of the ponies lasted the distance and the support party turned back, as planned, after the first month.

700-kilometre return journey into a completely unknown region of Antarctica would have been daunting enough. As things were, it seemed risky in the extreme. Mackay intimated as much in his diary, where he commented on the letters he left at the depot: 'These are last adieus, so they ought to be tragic.' Mawson, however, was pragmatic in his diary, giving no indication that their journey was entering its most vital and serious phase.

Their departure was delayed for two days by a blizzard so it was not until 16 December that they left the coast with rations for seven weeks, including 10 kilograms of seal liver and emperor penguin meat. It was an enormous relief to be travelling with just one sledge, albeit an overladen one, and not to have to put themselves through the physical and mental torment of relaying loads. They were less than halfway to the South Magnetic Pole as the skua flies, but because of relaying loads they had covered two-thirds of the total distance they would have to trek.

Despite having to haul only one sledge, neither the going nor the route-finding was easy. Each of them fell into hidden crevasses, and a famous anecdote relates that while Mawson was down a crevasse, dangling by the haul-line attached to the sledge and waiting for a rescue rope to be dropped to him, he hacked some interesting-looking ice-crystals from the wall of the crevasses and threw them up to the surface for later examination.

A succession of blizzards and days of strong winds slowed their progress even more. One blizzard was fierce enough to tear their tent in two places. With the fabric weakened, repairs and patching became frequent chores, and a very unpleasant one because sewing required removal of their warm wolf-skin mittens. Their goal was to achieve 16 kilometres per day during the inland, uphill journey, and 24 kilometres as they headed back to the coast. They pushed themselves very hard to achieve these targets.

On 27 December, below the slopes of Mt Larsen (at the head of the Larsen Glacier and the start of the polar plateau), they established a third depot, consisting of their ice-axes, alpine rope, ski boots, geological specimens, kerosene and a small amount of food. From here they had relatively good conditions underfoot and uncomplicated navigating, allowing them to meet their target distance virtually every day. However, the strain of the protracted journey on a poor diet was taking its toll, particularly on 50-year-old Edgeworth David. As they gained altitude the cold became more extreme, and Mawson suffered snow blindness in one eye and frostbite to his nose and cheek when he attempted to navigate through a blizzard. However, their determination to push on remained firm, and on 16 January 1909, they headed north-west from their tent to trudge the final 12 kilometres to the South Magnetic Pole. Mawson calculated their position, then they planted their flag and Edgeworth David took possession of the region for the British Crown. Mackay suggested three cheers for the King, a patriotic act which had not occurred to the two Australians. Mawson set up the camera, then after they bared their heads to the elements, Edgeworth David released the shutter with the aid of a piece of string. In his diary Mawson expresses no emotion about their achievement, but does note that at camp it was a beautifully still evening, and that all afternoon the temperature had stayed at -18°C.

For much of the return journey navigation was easy, as their outwards tracks were still visible in the snow. However, they had their share of blizzards, and hunger was a perpetual preoccupation. After months of sustained exertion in a cold climate on an inadequate diet, their physical condition was deteriorating rapidly. As Mawson noted on 30 January, 'It took the lot of us to make a whole man.' Some weeks

Although the flat sea-ice looks like easy travelling, salt in the surface snow made the snow stick to the sledge runners, making the sledges harder to haul. All three men would haul one of their two sledges then walk back to fetch the other one. Here Mackay, left, and Edgeworth David rest while Mawson takes a photo.

earlier Edgeworth David had reached his limits, but he pushed on almost as an automaton during the day, and bounced back, to an extent, to his vocal self at camp. He remained focused on the goal, but was unable to contribute nearly as much effort as Mawson or Mackay. Mawson became de facto leader, and on 31 January, with Mawson out of earshot, Mackay exerted his power as the party's doctor and threatened to declare the Professor insane unless he gave written authority of leadership to Mawson. Edgeworth David agreed immediately, but Mawson was horrified when he learnt about the incident. The leadership held no value for him and it was not the relationship he wished to have with his old professor.

All three men were falling apart mentally and physically, but Mawson had not perceived any sudden deterioration in the Professor's condition. Instead, he saw Mackay's coup as an act of desperation on what Mawson described as 'an awful day of despair, disappointment, hard travelling, agonising walking – forever falling down crevasses'. Low morale was to be expected, even though reaching the coast was now almost a certainty. A few days earlier Mackay had exploded when Mawson admitted to adding an extra sugar cube to the hoosh. This extravagance, fumed Scottish Mackay, was what was to be expected from a 'couple of foreigners'. He soon apologised, but his outburst was an indication of the pressure they were under, and that anything could be used as the beginning of an argument.

Although Mawson thought Mackay was overreacting, by 3 February he wrote in his diary that 'Prof was now certainly partially demented'. On that day they reached the open water of the Ross Sea, and set up camp because Mawson felt that for the moment Edgeworth David was incapable of continuing. At Mawson's suggestion they instigated four-hour watches in case the ship appeared. After one each – Mawson gave himself six-and-a-half hours – they were all sitting inside the tent for

The journey to the South Magnetic Pole, from Ross Island and back to the coast, was the longest unsupported sledge journey until the mid-1980s, when radios and air rescue were real possibilities. Mawson (right) set up this photo at what he had determined to be the Pole and Edgeworth David triggered the shutter with a length of string, which can be seen in the photo.

Luckily Shackleton's emergency plan for picking up the Magnetic Pole party along the Victoria Land coast worked because the timing happened to be right for both the ship and the shore party. No time was wasted while pulling Nimrod *up against the sea-ice when the shore party was sighted, which was just as well, because in his excitement Mawson had fallen down a crevasse and needed to be rescued.*

On the deck of Nimrod
*on the voyage home
from Antarctica,
Mawson looks
older than his
26 years. The harsh
Antarctic environment
has left him
weatherbeaten, but
also much wiser
about human nature.
On such demanding
and protracted
adventures the
true character of
everyone involved is
brought to the surface.*

the few minutes required to eat a meal when a gunshot cracked the silence. Mawson knocked over the stove, and the Professor, as he scrambled out of the tent with Mackay hot on his heels. A second shot rang out as they saw the bow of *Nimrod* appearing around the corner of the inlet. Mawson ran, waving and shouting, then suddenly broke through the snow-crust and dropped six metres into a hidden crevasse, landing hard on his back. Mackay and David were incapable of getting him out. This task was taken care of by the crew of the ship, which soon moored against the ice. J.K. Davis dropped down into the crevasse on the end of a rope to extricate Mawson, adding another bond to their developing friendship. This finale of Mawson's was a suitably dramatic ending to an extraordinary feat of endurance.

After collecting Edgeworth David, Mawson and Mackay, *Nimrod* returned to Cape Royds. Shackleton's party was also overdue. If faced with this scenario, Mawson had instructions to mount a search party but had not yet done so when Shackleton and Wild arrived on 28 February. They had turned around 160 kilometres from the Pole because to have gone any further would have meant not coming back. As it was, Marshall pushed himself to his absolute limit and was unable to complete the final haul to Base. Adams had remained with him to tend to his needs. Despite his weakened condition, and giving an example of leadership which no doubt impressed Mawson, Shackleton led Mackay, McGillain (a stoker from *Nimrod*) and Mawson south again to bring back Adams and Marshall. Mawson and Mackay had spent three weeks at Cape Royds recovering from their exhausting journey, but the rescue was still hard work, with temperatures becoming noticeably colder as summer drew to an end. Their mission had its exciting moments but was accomplished without major incident.

Years later in New Zealand, analysis of Mawson's calculations suggested that the party did not in fact reach the South Magnetic Pole. Unlike the South Pole, the Magnetic Pole is not a static feature, and the area where it lay had been incorrectly estimated by other magneticians and expeditions. The B.A.E. Northern Party reached the region indicated, but they were hampered by the fact that the journey to the Mag Pole was an afterthought on the part of Shackleton, and they were not adequately equipped to determine the Magnetic Pole's precise location. There was no subterfuge here, as according to their equipment and Mawson's calculations, they did reach the area of the South Magnetic Pole's oscillation. In Mackay's opinion, they had not reached the heart of the Magnetic

On the deck of Nimrod after their push to within 160 kilometres of the South Pole are, from left, Frank Wild, Shackleton, Eric Marshall and Jameson Adams. They had left Cape Royds on 13 October and their support party turned back on 7 November. On 25 November they passed Scott's furthest south. All their ponies died, leaving the men to be the beasts of burden, and it was fitting that they began to include pony food as part of their daily rations. A blizzard hit them on 30 December, followed by one on 7 January which lasted for 60 hours. On 9 January, frostbitten and starving, the four men claimed to have raised the flag at 88° 23' South. They took photographs, then retraced their steps 1050 kilometres back to Cape Royds, a journey which tested them to their limits. Recent evidence suggests Shackleton often added on a few miles each day to crack the "100 miles from the Pole" psychological barrier.

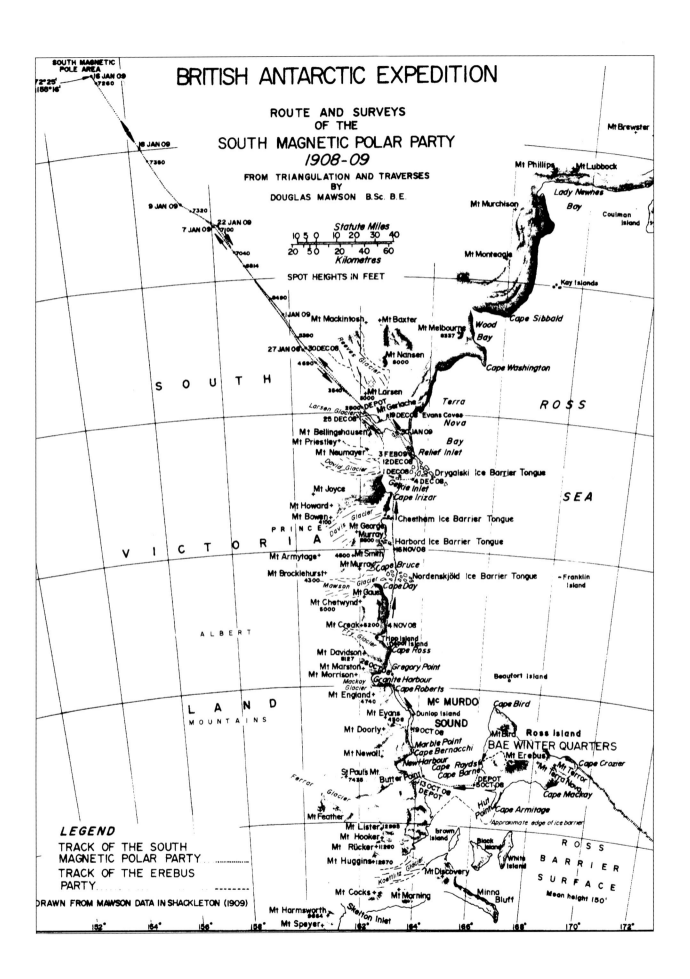

BRITISH ANTARCTIC EXPEDITION

ROUTE AND SURVEYS
OF THE
SOUTH MAGNETIC POLAR PARTY
1908-09
FROM TRIANGULATION AND TRAVERSES
BY
DOUGLAS MAWSON B.Sc. B.E.

Statute Miles

Kilometres

SPOT HEIGHTS IN FEET

LEGEND

TRACK OF THE SOUTH
MAGNETIC POLAR PARTY ....
TRACK OF THE EREBUS
PARTY .... -------

DRAWN FROM MAWSON DATA IN SHACKLETON (1909)

50

Pole area and it is possible that wishful thinking led Mawson to decide that near enough was good enough.

The quality of the rest of Mawson's scientific work on the B.A.E. has stood the test of time, as has this remarkable feat of endurance. The record they set for the longest unsupported sledge journey (measured from the depot established by motor car 24 kilometres from Cape Royds) lasted for almost 80 years. It was broken by Roger Mear, Robert Swan and Gareth Wood, who travelled 1405 kilometres from Ross Island to the South Pole in 1986. They had used skis, had accurate maps, lightweight clothing and equipment, as well as nutritious lightweight food. They also had a great deal more information about the Antarctic environment. Edgeworth David, Mawson and Mackay travelled 1265 kilometres from Cape Royds to the South Magnetic Pole area and back to the coast at Relief Inlet, but because they relayed their loads to Drygalski Glacier Tongue, they actually covered 2028 kilometres on foot. However, in the eyes of the rest of the world, their achievement was overshadowed by Shackleton's supported epic journey – which set its own records for endurance – a realm of endeavour which Shackleton was unwittingly to make his specialty.

Map of South Victoria Land, prepared by Mawson for use in Shackleton's book The Heart of the Antarctic *in 1909. This map is based on the version modified for the Jacka's edited* Mawson Antarctic Diaries *in 1988. The route of the Northern Party (as Shackleton officially called it) to the area of the South Magnetic Pole, based on Mawson's carto-graphic work. Mawson had also been designated responsible for making magnetic and geological surveys (which was supposed to extend to prospecting for two weeks in Dry Valley), and was made second-in-command of the party.*

CHAPTER 3

Coming

Of

Age

'Adelaide's hero, so good-looking and so much in demand', was how Paquita Delprat, Mawson's future wife remembered him in 1909. Although this portrait dates from a few years later, it captures something of Mawson's charisma.

Ernest Shackleton had invited Edgeworth David and Douglas Mawson on his expedition for pragmatic reasons. Yet in these two he had found much more than mere pawns in the political game of expedition fundraising. Edgeworth David was the senior member of an otherwise youthful team of men with varied temperaments and tolerances. The Professor was a good talker and a good listener with a genteel manner, a man to whom respect seemed a natural response – a useful commodity on a long and difficult Antarctic expedition. Shackleton's regard for Mawson is reflected by the tasks he delegated to him in Antarctica. Mawson was the photographer on the climb of Mt Erebus, which, given the cumbersome procedures and equipment of photography at the time and the likelihood of encountering both blizzards and molten rock, was a challenging assignment. On the Magnetic Pole journey he was made second-in-charge, as well as having the duties of navigating and mapping the terrain. He was also allocated the formidable task of searching for Shackleton and his companions should they not return from the South Pole. Shackleton obviously recognised Mawson as a man of strength as well as ability.

Mawson was to capitalise on the opportunities presented by his involvement with Antarctica, but at first he was surprised to the point of bewilderment by the heroes' welcome when the ship pulled into Sydney in late March 1909. Much of the attention was focused on Edgeworth David, through no doing of his own, and the Professor made efforts to direct the limelight towards his student, the man who had guided them to the Magnetic Pole and led them back safely. It was not until Mawson returned to Adelaide that he became the centre of adulation. When his train arrived at the station near the university, his carriage was mobbed by students and he was carried by a large crowd up to the university. One of his favourite photos in later years was of this spontaneous 'kidnapping', as the *Adelaide Advertiser* described the event.

As soon as he was able, Mawson returned to the university to his teaching work and his own studies. He was also keen to get back to his field work, particularly his ongoing studies in the Barrier Ranges across the border in New South Wales. During one field trip he visited nearby Broken Hill, where he had dinner with friends. Also present was Francesca 'Paquita' Delprat, who later became his wife. Paquita was the sixth child of G.D. Delprat, General Manager of BHP, whose family home was in Adelaide at the time. Mawson was immediately taken with Paquita, nine years his

junior. Although Mawson never wrote anything for public consumption to explain why he was drawn to Paquita, the success of their long marriage would indicate that they immediately recognised a kindred spirit in each other. And unknown to Mawson, Paquita had spotted him at a university sports event and was taken by his smile, directed not at her but unselfconsciously at friends. After their first meeting, their paths were not to cross again for some time, as Mawson was busily tying up loose ends, including completing his doctoral thesis, before heading to Europe in December of 1909, armed with several letters of introduction to some of Britain's most respected geologists. When in Britain, he also planned to catch up with John King Davis and hopefully meet Robert Falcon Scott, about whom he'd heard much from Shackleton, Wild and Joyce, and who, apparently, was organising another expedition to Antarctica.

Mawson's journey to Britain was uneventful, and there was plenty of time to brood on the possibility of returning to Antarctica. He was intrigued by the vast section of the continent to the south of Australia, in which no-one seemed to have any interest. In London he was quick to catch up with Davis, who showed him the sights. Mawson had no trouble arranging a meeting with Scott – news of his own achievements had preceded him in the form of a recommendation from Edgeworth David. Scott was indeed organising another expedition, and once again his interest was in reaching the South Pole. By this stage Mawson's interest had crystallised into

In Sydney in March 1909, Mawson felt uneasy at the official welcomes staged for the Australian members of the British Antarctic Expedition. At the first opportunity he caught a train to Adelaide and on arrival at Central Station was surprised to be greeted by an enthusiastic mob of colleagues and students, who carried him the short distance to the University of Adelaide. This was one of Mawson's favourite photographs. Straw hats identify students among the crowd; Mawson is obviously suntanned.

exploring the Antarctic coast south of Australia. He felt this enormous task could readily be commenced as part of Scott's expedition if he and a shore party were landed at Cape Adare, a finger-like peninsula marking the point where the Antarctic coastline makes an abrupt turn to the south to form the western shore of the Ross Sea. Scott had other ideas for Mawson. He offered him £800 pounds for the expedition, more if it was extended by 'circumstances', provided he join Scott as one of the three men to make the final push to the Pole. Mawson was a scientist, not a professional adventurer, and he stated again that he was more interested in exploring the northern coast.

Some weeks passed and neither man changed his point of view. This was when Douglas Mawson decided to take the enormous step of organising his own expedition. He had achieved much on the B.A.E. with Shackleton, but he realised how much more could have been done with a program of scientific research thoroughly planned in advance, particularly when this work was the expedition's primary goal.

Mawson accepted an invitation to dine with Scott and his wife Kathleen, with whom he felt an immediate rapport. Scott repeated his offer, and Mawson repeated his reply, confirming that he intended to work towards organising his own expedition. They parted on friendly terms, with Scott disappointed and Mawson a little daunted by the prospect of what he had decided to take on.

Mawson went to see Shackleton, now Sir Ernest, who was excited by his idea and promised to help raise funds. Mawson was a little wary of Shackleton's 'any means to an end' entrepreneurial approach to expedition organising – with good reason, as it turned out. Soon Shackleton decided that he should lead the expedition but that Mawson could set the scientific and exploratory agenda. Mawson tentatively accepted. He wished to explore the entire coastline from Cape Adare as far west as Gaussberg, a landmark mountain in a region south of the Indian Ocean that had been claimed for Germany by Eric von Drygalski in 1902. This vast region included all of the Antarctic coastline which lay to the south of Australia and a healthy margin to both the east and west. To accomplish this he intended to establish four separate land bases, one on Macquarie Island and three on the continent, each with its own scientific program as well as the capability of charting the coastline in both direction using sledges. One of these three bases would have the extra goal of sending a party to the Magnetic Pole again, so that Mawson could determine how much the Pole had moved in the three years between his visits. It was an audacious scheme, the like of which had never been contemplated, let alone attempted.

Paquita Delprat at around the time Mawson met her at Broken Hill in 1909, where she was holidaying. Her father was general manager for BHP. The Delprats lived in Adelaide, but moved to Melbourne in 1913.

Amidst making detailed plans, Mawson travelled to Hungary to assess the potential of some goldmines that Shackleton, always the entrepreneur, was looking at buying. Mawson took the opportunity of being in Europe to continue networking with Antarctic experts. In those days anyone who had been there qualified as an expert because so little was known about the frozen continent. Coincidentally, it was at this time that Mawson received a letter from his father, who was in New Guinea pursuing his own exotic dream, and who like his son, needed to raise money. Mawson was preoccupied and unable to help. With Shackleton's assistance the first sponsorship monies were pledged, but Mawson left Britain with only a quarter of his £40,000 budget accounted for. It was a promising beginning but a lot of work remained to be done.

Mawson returned to Australia in mid-1910, via the United States, and renewed his acquaintance with Paquita Delprat, who thought Mawson's interest in her 'seemed like a dream. He was so tall, so good-looking and so much in demand – Adelaide's hero'.

Amid his usual field work and on-campus duties, he had a busy schedule of publicising his vision of Antarctic exploration and presenting sponsorship proposals.

Mawson was a man who made the most of his opportunities. His explorations on Shackleton's expedition gave him rare knowledge of Antarctica, which he hoped to use as his entrée to prominent scientists in Britain. Here he is seen relaxing in a deckchair en route to London in December 1909. Already he was thinking of returning to Antarctica and was making plans to meet Robert Falcon Scott.

In London, Mawson met with Robert Falcon Scott and his wife Kathleen. He was offered a position not only as a member of Scott's upcoming journey to Antarctica, but also was invited to join the three-man team to make the final push to the South Pole. As Mawson's interest was in scientific study, he declined the offer, but he established what was to be a lifelong friendship with Kathleen Scott. This photo is taken on Terra Nova *shortly before Scott's departure on his final expedition. Sir Clements Markham, seated, was President of the Royal Geographical Society and championed good naval men such as Scott ahead of entrepreneurial Shackleton and colonial Mawson.*

The one proposal that was accepted almost immediately was his offer of marriage to Paquita. As she wrote in her biography of him: 'Although I did not in the least want Douglas to go to the Antarctic, when I realised that he was going whether I liked it or not, he had no keener supporter.'

In January 1911, a month after Paquita had accepted his proposal, Mawson returned to England because Shackleton had withdrawn from the expedition. Mawson was intent on securing the sponsorship which had been pledged when Shackleton was to be leader. But when he arrived in London he was dismayed to discover that most of these deals and had fallen through, and that Shackleton had actually received some of the money and spent it elsewhere. Mawson was in a desperate position, but was supported by John King Davis, who was to captain the ship – when they bought one.

At this time, the wealthiest men in Australia had sailed to England to attend the coronation of King George V. Mawson hoped that the emotional fervour of these patriotic celebrations would encourage a generous response from these Australians towards an expedition which would further the standing of both their own country and the British Empire. Using this line of persuasion he met with some success, but not as extensively as he had hoped. He saw that he would have to approach the British rich list as well. Mawson played up to the romantic notion of the tough but noble Antarctic explorer, and worked every contact as hard as he could. One meeting led to another, and he was passed up the social ladder, lunching with the aristocratic and the influential, many of whom, despite being wealthy, were generous only with good wishes and advice. He was annoyed to find that because he wasn't proposing to push for the Pole, people tended to be less interested in his upcoming expedition than in his past exploits.

However, the expedition's bank balance was gradually rising. After dinner with William Heinemann, publisher of Shackleton's book *Heart of the Antarctic*, he was offered an advance of £1000 for a book about the expedition. Donations of goods were pledged. The Royal Geographical Society gave a grant of £500, considerably less than he had hoped for. Between financial meetings Mawson was busily hunting for a ship. He and Davis eventually settled on *Aurora*, a Dundee whaler made in 1876, which had gained its polar credentials by rescuing the survivors of the Greely expedition to the Arctic. Mawson wondered where he was going to find £6000, the agreed price for the ship; expedition funds were accruing, but not fast enough. At

Mawson with Sir Ernest Shackleton in his Regent Street office shortly after arriving in London in 1910. Mawson spoke to Shackleton about his idea of mounting an expedition to the Antarctic coast west of the Ross Sea, the proposition which he had hoped that Scott would incorporate in his expedition. Shackleton showed more enthusiasm and suggested that he lead the expedition. He later lost interest but helped Mawson with his fundraising.

this time he wrote to Paquita, 'If you know me aright, you will understand that once having said I am intending to go to the Antarctic I shall go, even if it is in a whaleboat.'

Luckily he was able to galvanise Shackleton's enthusiasm again, perhaps through the tiniest sense of guilt, and a public appeal was launched with Sir Ernest's support. Donations began to roll in, and soon there was sufficient to buy the ship. More money would have been raised were it not for suggestions by influential supporters of Robert Scott that funds for Antarctic exploration should be directed to Scott. This was a strange request, given that Scott's final, ill-fated expedition was already well funded and had sailed south from New Zealand at the end of November 1910, ten weeks before Mawson arrived in England. This ungenerous attitude by the upper-crust Antarctic set was a sign of how some Britons still viewed Australians at the time. Ironically, Kathleen Scott offered Mawson her home as a base for his fundraising, as she saw that Mawson was pursuing the same cause as her husband. Not surprisingly, Mawson considered that staying in the Scotts' house would be an undiplomatic move. However, he did follow Kathleen's advice about aeroplanes. She encouraged him to take a monoplane to Antarctica, largely because of the publicity it would bring. She gave Mawson an introduction to an acquaintance

Mawson's friend and 1st Officer from Nimrod, John King Davis, helped Mawson locate a vessel capable of handling the difficult conditions likely to be encountered on Mawson's Australasian Antarctic Expedition. Mawson wanted Davis to captain the ship and be second in command of the expedition. Mawson was pleased that he was able to interest Frank Wild as well as he had been very impressed with Wild's unflappable nature during the 1901–04 Shackleton expedition.

of hers at Vickers, the aeroplane manufacturers, and the expedition was provided with a £1000 aircraft on credit.

London was also a good base for obtaining specialised equipment, much of which was stowed on the ship as soon as it was acquired. Mawson bought, borrowed or had donated sledges, skis, reindeer skin sleeping bags, finnesko (reindeer skin boots), wolf-skin mittens, burberry weatherproof suits, eight cameras and photograph plates, food, books, sundry equipment and 49 sledging dogs. As these animals would travel to Australia on board *Aurora*, he also signed on two dog-handlers, the aristocratic Lieutenant B.E.S. Ninnis and the Swiss Dr Xavier Mertz. As neither of these men had experience with sledge dogs or polar conditions, their choice for the job is puzzling. Mertz did have considerable skiing and mountaineering experience, qualifications which perhaps Mawson valued after his experiences climbing Mt Erebus without either.

Frank Wild, who had first been south with Scott in 1901–04, was also recruited in Britain. Mawson had got to know Wild well during his expedition with Shackleton, where Wild had proved himself on the push towards the Pole, and, perhaps more importantly, during the long winter in the cramped quarters of the hut. Dependable and unflappable, Mawson planned for Wild to be in charge of one of the three planned Antarctic bases. Also to travel to Australia on *Aurora* was F.H. Bickerton, an engineer who at age 22 was already a Fellow of the Royal Geographical Society.

With Shackleton's assistance, Mawson generated much newspaper publicity, which in turn helped with fundraising and the donation of goods. *Aurora* became an object for sightseeing, and one of the visitors was Anna Pavlova, the extraordinary Russian ballet dancer who was much fêted in London at the time. She brought a good luck gift for Mawson, a small golliwog wearing a colourful dress, which now resides in the Mawson Antarctic Collection in Adelaide. Russian legend has it that Mawson invited Pavlova to be godmother to the ship and that the arrangement was confirmed by the breaking of a bottle of champagne against the bow.

With the golliwog safely ensconced in his cabin, Mawson felt confident leaving the ship in charge of Captain Davis, so he returned to Australia, arriving in Adelaide in August 1911. He planned to sail south from Hobart in December, which gave him less than four months before an intended 15-month absence. In these four months he had to set his university life in order, obtain the majority of his provisions and equipment, finalise expedition members and load all the supplies onto the ship. And, of course, he needed to spend time with his fiancée. He spent his 'free' evenings with Paquita, but instead of flowers he arrived with lists. 'Such lists they were!' she wrote. 'Approximately 16 tons of food for a party of 12 men wintering for a year. This was to be supplemented by fresh penguin eggs and seal meat, where procurable. Vegetables, cereals, dried fruits and jam. Milk, butter, cheese; and soaps, pickles, tea and coffee, etc, etc.' And these were only the lists for the largest of the three planned continental parties.

In many ways, less could be achieved in four months in 1911 than can be now. Communication was not instantaneous, and goods were transported by horse and cart. Mawson made frequent use of telegrams and delegated large tasks to expedition members, once he had selected them. Even so, he didn't have a spare moment, and Paquita wrote of him growing thinner and thinner as the months went by.

The most pressing matter was raising the balance of the £48,000 needed to finance the expedition. Although the Australasian Antarctic Expedition was a private exploration and research expedition, several state governments came to Mawson's aid with grants, as did the federal government and the Australian Association for the Advancement of Science. Mawson was to sail from Hobart with debts, but ones that he considered manageable. An added distraction was the crash of the expedition aeroplane, which Watkins had travelled with to Australia from Britain. At a publicity flight in Adelaide the plane had faltered and crashed. Frank Wild, who was the passenger, crawled out of the wreckage with only sprains and bruises. The machine was no longer airworthy, and would have cost too much and taken too long to repair. But the engine was in workable order so Mawson decided to take the machine south where it could be adapted into an 'air tractor' for hauling loads.

In determining his team, Mawson was guided by his instincts, and perhaps by Shackleton's unconventional wisdom. He needed men with the spirit to endure firstly the worst ocean conditions on Earth, followed by the most inhospitable climate on Earth, much of it to be spent in semi-darkness. But his team needed more

Mawson inspects Aurora *in London in 1911, having purchased it sight unseen at a good price. Davis recommended the whaling ship, built in 1876, which had gained its polar credentials in 1883 by rescuing the survivors of the Greely expedition to the Arctic. When the expedition's relief ship failed to arrive, and in the absence of all other food, the first men to die were eaten by the others. Six of the 24 expeditioners survived for two years until rescued by* Aurora.

than just the ability to endure, as he wanted daily scientific work conducted. Of course, there were definite skills required, but skills were worth nothing to Mawson if he perceived a quirk of character which might threaten the applicant's performance or disrupt that of others. He sought young enthusiastic men who were practical as well as scholarly. Like Shackleton, Mawson took notice of those who showed initiative in applying for a place on the expedition. Frank Hurley was assured of a position from the moment Mawson realised that the young photographer, in order to plead his case, had bribed a conductor to be allowed to share a railway carriage with him. Hurley certainly proved himself to be a valuable team member on this and many other great adventures.

Another team member, Charles Laseron, provides insight into Mawson's selection process. In his interview, the nervous Laseron was asked not about his qualifications as a collector of marine specimens but whether he could cook. Laseron admitted to having made dampers on various camping excursions 'but confessed that my first efforts were probably still in the bush in a state of semi-petrification. For some reason this answer seemed to please him, but after a very short interview I was dismissed.' Rather than receiving a formal invitation to join the team, Laseron was sent a letter asking him to look up Mawson's contact at the Australian Museum and from him learn the art of taxidermy.

Laseron, like the other young men Mawson engaged, found that every spare moment until the departure of the expedition was devoted to the gathering of stores and equipment to be shipped to Hobart. The organisation involved was greater than any Antarctic expedition to date because four different bases, rather than one or two, were to be set up, including a base on Macquarie Island, from where it was hoped radio messages would be relayed from Antarctica to Australia. Supplies had to be stowed base by base in case rough seas or poor anchorages demanded rapid unloading.

Twenty-three-year-old Lieutenant Belgrave Ninnis enjoying the sunshine on board Aurora *on its voyage from London to Sydney. His father, Inspector-General R.N. Ninnis, had been part of the Alert and Discovery Arctic Expedition. Ninnis, with Swiss ski champion Xavier Mertz, was in charge of the Greenland huskies on the voyage and in Antarctica.*

It was in Hobart in late November that the 31 members of the landing parties met each other for the first time. Wild, Bickerton, Ninnis and Mertz had travelled from Britain, and Eric Webb and Dr L.A. Whetter had sailed across from New Zealand. The rest of the team were Australia-based if not Australian. As Antarctic veterans, Mawson and Wild were regarded with awe, as was Captain Davis. But Mawson was exhausted. He had received a magnificent send-off at the Town Hall in Adelaide by the State Governor, Sir Hort Day Bosanquet, the Chief Justice, Sir Samuel Way, the Chief Secretary, the City Mayor and other luminaries. Mawson stated that 'I am prepared to go on exploring for the rest of time, but it is the organisation from which one shrinks'.

In his final words to his home crowd he said: 'Most of the speakers have referred to myself, and I appear to be chief spirit in this expedition. To some extent that is so. Everything depends on the personnel of the expedition. But I am only one of 31 of the land party...You will know in 18 months' time who have been the successful members of the expedition and who have not. I personally feel that all the men chosen will be successful.'

Douglas Mawson had given everything in his power to make his vision a reality. Raw curiosity about a huge blank on the map had grown into a loaded ship, an excited crew, inspired expeditioners and myriad plans. But the hardest work, and the hardship, were just about to begin.

Mawson, wearing a hat, on the deck of Aurora *during the loading of the ship at Queen's Wharf, Hobart, in November 1911. The ship arrived from England at the end of October and, with Frank Wild in charge of the stores, a busy month was spent on final preparations for the long journey south.*

CHAPTER 4

South
On Aurora

Among the guests on board Aurora *on the day of
departure from Hobart were Tasmania's Premier
Sir Elliot Lewis and Governor Sir Harry Barron,
who relayed best wishes from the royal family.
Mawson, however, had not officially been granted
powers to claim land for the British Crown.
Thousands of folk packed Queen's Wharf to
farewell the Australasian Antarctic Expedition
on 2 December 1911.*

When the fully laden *Aurora* was ready to depart from Hobart on 2 December 1911, a large supply of provisions and equipment remained stacked inside the expedition warehouse. At Queen's Wharf a crowd of thousands, including Tasmania's Premier Sir Elliot Lewis, and Governor Sir Harry Barron, farewelled the ship. Among those who waved from the dock as the ship pulled away were 20 expedition members, all with broad smiles on their faces. Everything was going according to plan – their turn to leave would come soon. The essential supplies for life, exploration and scientific work for 31 men for 15 months had occupied more space than the *Aurora* could accommodate, so Mawson had chartered the small steamer *Toroa* to leave six days after *Aurora,* carrying extra coal, the remaining supplies, and the rest of the expedition team as far as Macquarie Island. The departures were staggered to allow *Aurora* time to locate a suitable site for the Macquarie Island base. There was no sheltered harbour at the island, and in the fierce conditions of the Southern Ocean it was prudent to minimise anchorage time offshore.

Everyone on board *Aurora* quickly became aware that the voyage south was to be no picnic. No sooner was Tasmania out of sight than they were hit by a four-day

Johnnie Hunter reading the deep-sea thermometer attached to a water bottle recovered from deep sounding during Aurora's *first voyage south. Captain Davis is standing upright.*

The capture of biological specimens was an important part of the expedition's work. Here Stillwell (left), Harrisson, Hunter show the size of an albatross on the deck of Aurora.

gale. Huge waves crashed against the ship and across the deck. Half the bridge was washed away, and the starboard bulwarks were damaged, as were the expedition's motorboat and the air tractor. Other equipment lashed to the deck was spared, including prefabricated sections of the expedition huts and cans of fuel. Mawson and others were seasick, but when the storm abated seasickness didn't bother Mawson again.

Nine days after leaving Hobart, *Aurora* reached Macquarie Island. The expeditioners first landed at Caroline Cove, near the southern end of the island, where an afternoon was spent exploring. After the rough passage from Tasmania, everyone was pleased to get ashore. The next day, *Aurora* steamed up the east coast and around the northern tip of the island to anchor in the shelter of a bay formed by the peninsula of the island's north head. Here they found a few sealers, stranded for the summer after their ship had been lost, who were collecting seal blubber and penguin oil.

For most of the men on *Aurora*, Macquarie Island was their introduction to penguins, skua gulls and elephant seals, forms of wildlife typical of Antarctic waters, even though Macquarie Island's latitude of 55°S was well north of the Antarctic Circle. Once on shore Frank Hurley found himself surrounded by photographic opportunities, and he suddenly realised that he'd left an essential lens back at

Caroline Bay, their first landing point. With Mawson's permission he set off on a five-day trek to the far end of the island, with Hutchinson, a sealer, as his guide and Harrisson providing safety in numbers.

Meanwhile, *Toroa* had arrived with the remaining expeditioners. The Greenland dogs were given a break from shipboard life and 50 sheep were brought ashore to graze. Supplies for the team for the forthcoming year were unloaded onto the beach of the isthmus that led from the main section of the island to its north head. *Toroa* was now ready to leave, and the stranded crew of the sealing vessel *Clyde* which had been shipwrecked a month earlier were delighted to clamber on board. The shipwrecked sealers paid the expedition for the storage of the seal oil they had planned to take home on their own ship. It was an example of an ill wind blowing good, for Mawson at least, as this covered the cost of chartering *Toroa*.

The base took two weeks to construct and stock, with Mawson setting the example of long days of hard work. He made no entries in his diary during the stay on the island, being preoccupied with co-ordinating all the tasks which had to be done before *Aurora* continued south. However, he did find the odd moment to revel in new, exciting horizons. 'I stood looking out to the sea one evening,' he later wrote, 'soon after sunset, the launch lazily rolling in the swell, and *Aurora* in the offing, while rich tints of the afterglow paled in the south-west. It was a soul-stirring evening.'

Given the stormy climate of Macquarie Island, the site at the northern end of the island was relatively accessible as it could be approached from the east or the west, depending on the prevailing winds. The peninsula rising above the isthmus seemed an ideal place to rig the wireless antenna, particularly because the sealers had already set up a flying fox here to move their blubber and oil barrels away from the wave-swept coast. The flying fox was in a state of disrepair, but was quickly strengthened. As radio communication was to be one of the main roles of this base, a large antenna had been brought and was duly assembled, under the watchful eyes of the operators – Charles Sandell from the Commonwealth Telegraph Office and Arthur Sawyer from the Australian Wireless Company. Other members of the Macquarie base were Leslie Blake (geologist and surveyor), New Zealander Harold Hamilton (zoologist), and George Ainsworth (meteorologist and base leader) who was on loan from the Commonwealth Meteorological Bureau.

The schooner Clyde *was shipwrecked on Nuggets Beach a month before* Aurora *arrived at Macquarie Island. The expedition was able to send the crew back to Australia on the supply ship* Toroa.

From Mawson's point of view, the most important function of the Macquarie Island base was the relaying of wireless messages from Antarctica to Australia. For this to be achieved, elaborate aerials were constructed on what became known as Wireless Hill. Messages were received from Australia but when forwarded were not received at Cape Denison.

Arthur Sawyer, biologist with the Macquarie Island team, examines a very relaxed elephant seal. The sealing industry had almost destroyed the fur seal colonies on Macquarie Island, and penguins and elephant seals were also threatened. Mawson lobbied strongly to have the island made into a nature reserve, where these industries could at least be regulated.

The process of constructing the expedition hut and erecting the wireless masts on the isthmus was seen as good practice for setting up the bases on the Antarctic continent, where conditions would be much harsher. At last most of the work was done – the remaining tasks could be left to the Macquarie Island team, and it was time to bring tools, tents and animals back on board and wave goodbye. The ship pulled into Caroline Cove to take on fresh water, but it took some time to find a source that was not contaminated by the surrounding penguin rookeries. The men would have preferred a more relaxing departure, as it was Christmas Day. However, there was time for a low-key celebration on board as the ship pulled away from the island.

With the first of his four planned bases successfully established, it must have been with a feeling of satisfaction and relief that Mawson asked Davis to head south for Antarctica, although the only entries in his diary for this period are very brief, mere records of fact. Good weather saw them make rapid progress on a course due south, rather than south-south-east towards Cape Adare. While still in England, Mawson had been annoyed to learn that Captain Scott had changed his plans and landed a party at Cape Adare, despite having had written notice of Mawson's intentions to begin his explorations of the north coast from a base at the cape. When Mawson

heard this news, Kathleen Scott had encouraged him to accept that it was unexpected circumstances, not premeditated plans, that had led Scott to change the location of his second base. Shackleton had faced a similar situation when he had reluctantly established his winter quarters near Scott's base on Ross Island. For Mawson, of course, there were many thousands of kilometres of completely unmapped coastline where he could set his bases, but Cape Adare had appeal because it was known to have an accessible rocky peninsula suitable for overwintering. No doubt there was a sense of security in starting such a bold venture from what was, relatively speaking, known ground. This was, after all, the first expedition that Mawson had organised and led, and the responsibilities and uncertainties must have weighed upon him heavily.

On 29 December, *Aurora* encountered chunks of floating ice and soon, through the mist, the first iceberg appeared. At midnight there was enough daylight to read by, and the expeditioners were excited by these portents of Antarctica. Each of the few vessels to visit this region had been unable to reach the continent because of dense pack-ice. The US sailor Charles Wilkes had made several sightings of land in

Rugged treeless hills typical of Macquarie Island rise behind an old sealers' hut at Lusitania Bay. During their stay on the island, Ainsworth's team 'renovated' the hut and then used it as a base while they surveyed the southern half of the island.

Frank Hurley's enthusiasm showed no bounds, particularly went it came to photography. Here he is seen at work on Aurora's *martingale, taking film of the ship's bow pushing through the pack-ice.*

these waters. Mawson had Wilkes' account with him, but as *Aurora* passed the first of the latitudes and longitudes where the American had sighted land they saw nothing but pack-ice. Mawson concluded in this instance that what Wilkes had thought was mountainous land must have been distant icebergs. The ship continued west along the still impenetrable pack-ice, and Mawson began to worry that unless they established a base soon, not only would the South Magnetic Pole be beyond sledging distance, but Macquarie Island would also be out of the range of their wireless transmitter. His grand scheme was threatened before they had even properly arrived.

On 3 January they sighted a huge ice wall, reminiscent of the Great Ice Barrier which stretched across the Ross Sea, and over which Shackleton had sledged towards the South Pole while Mawson had headed for the Magnetic Pole. Davis took the ship along the ice wall to the south-west until suddenly it turned south-east, leading *Aurora* into what everyone assumed was a huge bay. As they headed across the open water a blizzard blew in, and they were forced to shelter in the lee of a huge iceberg. When the wind dropped the next day they steamed parallel to what everyone thought was a continuation of the ice barrier. (However, when Aurora returned the next year this ice wall had vanished – it had been a 65-kilometre wide iceberg.) Beyond this monstrous berg Davis took the ship cautiously into the mist, steering carefully among icebergs and pack-ice. The ship's battle to break through the pack-ice had extended into its second week, and with only endless pack found in those places where Wilkes had recorded land, Mawson feared that heavy ice conditions this season – or the apparently endless ice cliffs rising direct from the sea – might prevent them from landing on the continent at all. If this happened, his years of work and the enormous financial commitments he had made would come to nothing, and he'd return home to financial ruin.

Yet there was an indefinable feeling on board that land was close at hand, and the deck was crowded with expeditioners keen for the first sighting. Close to midnight on 6 January, ice cliffs were seen ahead of the ship, and then beyond and above the mist loomed the outline of a huge dome of ice, rising an estimated 500 metres above the ocean. The expedition had arrived at the Antarctic continent. Black patches of rock were visible at sea level at the base of the ice cliffs, but the ice plateau remained inaccessible.

For Mawson it was a relief to reach the coast at last, but no doubt he remembered how, when he had been with Shackleton in the Ross Sea, *Nimrod* had been forced

Pack-ice stretching to the horizon, seen from the prow of Aurora *on 31 December 1911. Most of the expeditioners were newcomers to Antarctica and were fascinated by the sight which aroused only anxiety in Mawson. He was worried, justly as it turned out, that the pack-ice would prevent the ship from landing his three planned base parties.*

to travel hundreds of kilometres west – to Ross Island – from their intended landing site because of the unscalable ice cliffs of the Great Barrier. The ice cliffs here looked equally forbidding, and Mawson sensed that any landings along this coast would be difficult, dangerous and time-consuming – if possible at all. With these worries and limitations, he decided to modify his plan. Rather than establishing three shore bases, they would unload equipment, provisions and men for two bases at the first suitable landing site and establish one large base there. Captain Davis would then continue steaming west with Wild and his team in search of a second location.

The next day the expeditioners saw small rocky islands, alive with Weddell seals and Adelie penguins. On 8 January the first possibility for the main base presented itself. Into the wide scoop of what was soon named Commonwealth Bay protruded a rocky cape. Small islets warned Captain Davis against venturing within one nautical mile of the coast, so a whaleboat was put over the side and they rowed towards the shore. Cape Denison, as they called it, was dinted by a miniature harbour, which offered a sheltered landing place for the whaleboat. The sun shone brightly when Mawson, Wild and others pulled into the harbour and stepped ashore, and thus became the first people to land on the Antarctic continent between Cape Adare and Gaussberg, a distance of more than 3000 kilometres.

A quick exploration of the rocky area showed that, topographically at least, it was the ideal site to set up a base. Mawson thought of the place as an oasis, because in both directions and as far as the eye could see, insurmountable ice cliffs rose from the water's edge. The inland limits of the rocky area, less than a kilometre from the shore, gave straightforward access to apparently crevasse-free ice slopes leading up to an ice plateau. On the islets and the rocky shores of the cape itself there were seals and penguins enough to keep the biologists happy, the larder topped up and the dogs well fed. Around the cape the water was shallow – for dredging and fish-trapping – and as an unvisited coastline, the region was a new frontier for geology and meteorology; particularly the latter, as they were soon to discover. The site's one obvious shortcoming was that there was no solid sea-ice extending from the land into deep water. If there had been, all supplies could have been unloaded directly onto the sea-ice and then sledged to the shore. As it was, all supplies would have to be ferried ashore on their motor launch and the two whaleboats.

When they returned to the ship at 8 pm Mawson had already made his decision. The whaleboat was loaded with perishable supplies and was towed – by the motor

Severe conditions indeed were required to prevent Frank Hurley from taking photographs. Here he is seen washing cinematograph film in the sea after developing it on board Aurora. *Or perhaps this a posed shot set up by Hurley to show the drama of the photographic process in Antarctica, as he was the kind of man not always content to be behind the camera.*

Mawson was desperately worried that pack-ice and steep ice cliffs would prevent them from landing on the continent when, in early January 1912, they spotted a rocky cape in an open bay. After scouting the location by whaleboat Mawson quickly decided that this would be the site of the expedition's Main Base. Shallow water and rocky islets nearby meant that Aurora *had to anchor off shore, as shown here, with all supplies being brought ashore by boat.*

launch, similarly loaded – back to Boat Harbour. The weather suddenly changed for the worse as they approached the harbour. Everyone was underdressed for the sudden blizzard, so they unloaded as quickly as they could. Even so, Hoadley had three fingers frostbitten. This was the first of several adventures during more than a week of unloading of supplies. The most dramatic of these was when the launch was blown towards exposed rocks by fierce winds as the three men on board attempted to steer, bail and restart the engine at the same time.

Although the expedition was scheduled to spend a year here, a two-year supply of food was brought ashore as backup. There were also 23 tonnes of coal unloaded, as well as liquid fuels, huts, tools, wireless masts and scientific equipment. Such a huge job demanded an efficient approach. At first, the motor launch hauled the ship's two whaleboats fully laden, but in order to maximise the amount of equipment transferred on each trip, the sailors built rafts which could be towed behind the last whaleboat. Mawson noted about this process, 'Some of the sailors, while engaged in building rafts beside the ship were capsized into the water; after that the occupation was not a popular one.'

Cumbersome items such as the air tractor were lifted ashore with a derrick, which Frank Wild had improvised from the wireless masts. The unloading was frequently interrupted by bad weather, sometimes for more than a day at a time, so it was not until 19 January that the ship was ready to depart with the urgent task of depositing Frank Wild and his party at least 600 kilometres to the west.

But first, formalities were in order. A farewell party was held in the wardroom, with toasts being drunk from a historic bottle of Madeira, which had been presented to Davis in England with instructions to it take on its second journey to Antarctica. The wine's first visit, in 1874, had been when its previous owner, J.T. Buchanan, had taken it on board *Challenger* during that ship's circumnavigation of the world between 1872 and 1876. This Royal Society-sponsored research expedition had founded the modern science of oceanography, and so as a man of science, Mawson could have had no greater drop with which to celebrate the start of the most important phase of his expedition.

After discussing plans at length with Mawson, Captain Davis took *Aurora* west, keeping a course eight kilometres offshore. He passed Durmont d'Urville's Terre Adelie, where the Frenchman had landed on an island in 1840, then skirted north around pack-ice before heading south again as the floating ice cover became less dense. On 20 January he sailed directly over the point Wilkes had erroneously charted as Cape Carr. As a fellow sailor, Davis appreciated the risks that Wilkes had taken. If several of the American's sightings of land were wrong, he had at least determined the extent of dense pack-ice along the coast, and in recognition of his endeavour 70 years earlier Davis named the coast Wilkes Land.

Storms drove the ship north for several days, and when Davis was able to turn *Aurora* to the south again, he sailed once more over land that did not exist in its charted position, this time the Sabrina Coast, named by British sealer John Balleny in 1839. Davis' efforts to push south were rebuffed convincingly when he came to a huge ice wall. To make progress to the west, he was forced to follow the ice-wall north-west. It proved to be another massive glacial extension, which he named Termination Ice Tongue. They rounded the tongue's northerly limits and were then able to head further west in relatively open water. Mawson subsequently named this region the Davis Sea.

Captain Davis realised that Termination Ice Tongue protruded from a vast sheet of ice, which he named the Shackleton Ice Shelf as it was discovered on his birthday. As far as could be seen to the west, access to the ice-covered land was blocked by either the ice shelf or dense pack-ice. They were now only 200 kilometres east

At Cape Denison, the site of Mawson's main base, it was a huge job to transfer equipment and supplies for 18 men for a year from ship to shore. Here hut timbers are dragged 300 metres from the edge of the sea-ice at Boat Harbour to the site of the hut among the rock outcrops, having been unloaded at the water's edge by the derrick that Wild improvised out of radio masts.

of where Drygalski's expedition had unintentionally spent the winter of 1902–02 when their ship *Gauss* was frozen into the pack-ice. Mawson had not wanted Davis to explore beyond this region. This consideration, combined with the fact that *Aurora*'s coal supplies were now running low, made Davis anxious to head back to Hobart.

On 13 February, he took the ship up against the sea-ice, and Frank Wild, Harrisson and Hoadley walked across to the ice-cliffs of the Shackleton Ice Shelf. Here they found snow ramps which provided steep but comparatively straightforward access to the top of the ice shelf. After a quick look around on top, Wild decided that this would be their home for the next year, even though it was 40 kilometres from the continent. It was a bold decision, as at some point in the future the ice would break away from the shelf – and there was a chance it would happen while the seven expeditioners were on it. Yet this was their first and only opportunity to set up a base, so they took the risk of being marooned on a giant iceberg. The task of unloading supplies onto the sea-ice was tackled with gusto, as was the task of getting them to the top of the ice cliff, using a flying fox rigged from an

With no land predators to fear, Adelie penguins were more confused than frightened by Hunter's antics at Cape Denison.

To the east (shown here) and west of Cape Denison, ice-cliffs lined the seaward edge of the vast ice-sheets that dropped from the inland ice-plateau. Safe access inland was impossible everywhere at except at Cape Denison, and its discovery saved the expedition from failure.

Tracks of the S.Y. Aurora *on three Antarctic voyages, prepared by Mawson for use in the scientific report in 1942. This map is based on the version modified for the Jacka's edited* Mawson's Antarctic Diaries *in 1988.*

anchor in the ice to a makeshift gantry at the top of the cliff. Davis was nervous about this arrangement and he requested a letter from Wild removing all responsibility from him for the set-up. All went well, however, and by 21 February all the supplies were unloaded and all the farewells were made. From the bridge of *Aurora*, Wild's small party waving goodbye from the sea-ice looked much more lonely and vulnerable than the last view of Mawson and his team at Commonwealth Bay had looked. The ship began its long journey home. By this time of year, each night held a few hours of darkness, each of which hid an unknown number of icebergs. Gingerly, *Aurora* made its way to the north, out of the iceberg zone, and set a course for Hobart. Mawson and his teams now had a vast section of unknown Antarctica entirely to themselves.

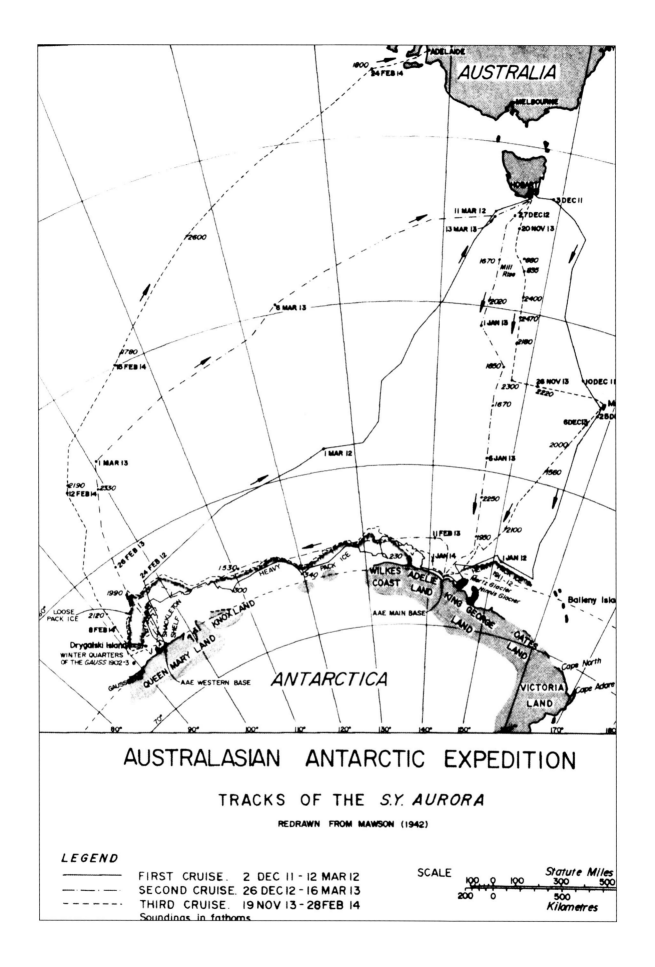

AUSTRALIA

ADELAIDE
1900
24 FEB 14
MELBOURNE

HOBART
3 DEC 11
11 MAR 12
13 MAR 13
27 DEC 12
20 NOV 13

2600

1670
Mill
Rise
990
835

6 MAR 13
2020
2400
11 JAN 13
2470
2180
1780
16 FEB 14
1850
2300
1670
26 NOV 13
2220
10 DEC 11

2190
1 MAR 13
2330
1 MAR 12
6 JAN 13
4560
6 DEC 11
28 D
2000
12 FEB 14
28 FEB 13
24 FEB 12
1 FEB 13
230
2250
1950
2100
1 JAN 14
1 JAN 12

1530
HEAVY
PACK ICE
540
WILKES
COAST
ADELIE
LAND
Jan 11-12
Mertz Glacier
Ninnis Glacier
Balleny Isla
1990
AAE MAIN BASE
KING GEORGE LAND
LOOSE
PACK ICE
2120
SHACKLETON SHELF
KNOX LAND
GATES
LAND
Cape North
8 FEB 14
Drygalski Island
QUEEN MARY LAND
VICTORIA
LAND
Cape Adare
WINTER QUARTERS
OF THE GAUSS 1902-3
GAUSS
AAE WESTERN BASE
ANTARCTICA

80°   90°   100°   110°   120°   130°   140°   150°   160°   170°   180°

AUSTRALASIAN ANTARCTIC EXPEDITION

TRACKS OF THE S.Y. AURORA

REDRAWN FROM MAWSON (1942)

LEGEND

——————— FIRST CRUISE. 2 DEC 11 – 12 MAR 12
—·—·—·— SECOND CRUISE. 26 DEC 12 – 16 MAR 13
— — — — THIRD CRUISE. 19 NOV 13 – 28 FEB 14
Soundings in fathoms

SCALE

Statute Miles
100   0   100   300   500
200   0   500
Kilometres

CHAPTER 5

The Windiest Place *in* *the* World

Hurley has been suspected of manipulating two photographs to create this spectacular image. Such ice caves do exist, however, and this one is just beyond John-O-Groats, as Mawson named the western limits of the exposed rock at Cape Denison. Although proudly Australian, Mawson's connection with the 'Old Country' is apparent in his names of landmarks, with John-O-Groats being the north-eastern shore of Scotland, and Land's End being the south-westerly point of both England and Cape Denison.

'Within a gunshot is the greatest glacier tongue yet known to the world,' wrote Mawson to his fiancée about their arrival at Commonwealth Bay. 'No human eyes have scanned it before ours – the feeling is magical. Young men whom you would scarce expect to be affected, stand half-clad without feeling the cold of the keen blizzard wind and literally dance from sheer exultation.'

Paquita Delprat wouldn't receive this letter for over a year because *Aurora* had left Commonwealth Bay before it was written. Unable to share his feelings with her as events happened, Mawson stored them in letter after letter, intending to hand-deliver them when he returned on *Aurora* the following year. In the first of these he wrote, 'Perhaps it is your love warmth that already shades me from cold, for I doubt I feel it as much as last time.'

Mawson's excitement at Commonwealth Bay was as great as anyone's, and it was with great gusto that he embraced the task of building the main party's winter quarters at Cape Denison. All the expeditioners with him were glad to be on land at last and were inspired by the energy of their leader, a man who tackled every task he expected his men to do.

The 18 men had originally been equipped and provisioned to operate as two separate parties, so there was considerable duplication of food and equipment.

In coastal Antarctica, exposed rock is prime real estate, not only for geologists but also for penguins and other birds, which need rocky areas to nest upon. Mawson, who is shown in this photograph to give scale to the outcrop of wind-eroded gneiss, found plenty of scope for geologising at Cape Denison. It was just as well, because inland lay endless expanses of ice and snow, with only the very tips of buried mountains poking through the ice.

On 30 January 1912, the hut was ready for occupation. Mawson made a speech and the Union Jack and the Australian flag were hoisted, then Mawson took possession of this part of Adelie Land for the King and the British Empire. As Laseron wrote, 'We gave three cheers, then put our helmets on as quickly as we could, for a nasty wind was blowing that nipped our ears.' The wind and perpetual cold are aspects of Antarctica not always conveyed in photos. The region was later named King George Land, with Adelie Land lying to the west.

Obvious examples were the two base huts, which Mawson decided should be joined together, with the small hut (set up as a workshop and storeroom) adjoining the second slightly larger hut (their living area). Secure shelter was the highest priority, so they worked 16 hours a day until the hut was built. Meanwhile they slept in a shanty town of wooden boxes, with the big air tractor crates forming the roof. Those who didn't fit inside pitched expedition pyramid tents nearby.

The hut was constructed about 40 metres from the shore of Boat Harbour, but the site was actually much further from the water, as the sea-ice extended another 250 metres into the harbour. In order to blast holes in the rock for foundation posts, dynamite was first warmed in the pocket of somebody's jacket. A solid frame was attached to the foundation posts, and while the floor was being laid and wall boards nailed, 50 tonnes of rocks were bolstered around the foundations. This was particularly hard work, and it made for good sleep, both at the end of the day and during the winter blizzards, as everyone had confidence the hut wouldn't blow away. The working conditions were difficult because of the cold and wind but there was much amusement at the endless parade of mishaps. As the roof neared completion, Frank Bickerton was nailing the roofing from above when his work was interrupted by 'Dad' McLean sliding off the roof in dramatic fashion, taking the stove chimney with him. Bickerton opted for a more secure work position, and sat down to continue his hammering, but at that moment Xavier Mertz, who was zealously nailing up ceiling boards from inside, missed the roof beam with his nail and instead found Bickerton's backside. Mawson summarised the incident, noting that 'individuals sitting on the roof were sometimes observed to start up suddenly and temporarily lose interest in the work'.

Surprisingly, there were no serious accidents, apart from Hunter, who needed stitches in two fingers after crushing them under a heavy case.

When the time came to fit out the interior of the huts a crucial part of the stove appeared to be missing. The theory put forward was that the missing parts could only be in the single crate which, during unloading, had been mishandled and dropped into the bay. Mawson and Charles Laseron equipped themselves with a whaleboat and a variety of devices with hooks and set off to retrieve it, but although could they see the crate, they were unable to bring it to the surface. 'There's only

The raising of the wireless masts was an important event, as Mawson wanted to be the first to broadcast and receive wireless messages in Antarctica, not because he wanted to be in the record books but because he wanted to extend the limits of this still new invention. During the first year in Antarctica they received no messages from Macquarie Island, so they didn't find out until the return of Aurora *that some of their transmissions were received and relayed to Australia.*

It would have been possible to have brought enough ready-made food bags, but Mawson knew that it was essential for the men to have plenty of jobs to keep them busy during the winter. Here Hurley gets ahead with his chores during autumn, perhaps to give himself more time for the practical jokes for which he became famous as winter progressed. Beside him are boxes of cut blubber for the dogs.

one thing for it,' said Mawson, and he stripped off and jumped over the side. He could just reach the crate while keeping his head above water so he heaved it aboard, hauled himself out of the water, and, as he put it, 'established a new record for myself in dressing'.

The crate proved to be full of jam and the missing stove parts were eventually found elsewhere, but the incident demonstrated to the men that the call of duty, which needed to be answered, could take unexpected directions in Antarctica.

The living quarters were 7.3 metres square, with pairs of bunks around the walls and a cubicle 2 metres square for Mawson. At the opposite end was the kitchen area, with the darkroom (or more accurately, dark-alcove) in the corner. A large table and benches took up most of the floor space in the middle of the room and above the

Mawson had brought many sets of skis from Norway and some from Australia, as well as a ski champion who could teach everyone how to use them. However, the icy conditions close to Cape Denison were not ideal. As Laseron wrote, 'Walter Hannam, with his seventeen stone (108 kg), partially solved the problem by using skis as a sledge on which he lay full length; and great was the delight of all when they separated from beneath him and he continued on his way for a considerable distance before he could pull up.' The sky-larking of the men led Mawson to ask Xavier Mertz to stop giving lessons as he feared serious injuries might result.

table an acetylene generator was rigged up to provide light. A door next to the kitchen bench led into the workshop, which housed the wireless equipment, complete with a petrol motor and generator, as well as a lathe, another stove, a carpentry bench and a bench where the scientists could work on their specimens. In describing the workroom, Laseron wrote, 'if the desire had come to swing the proverbial cat, it would have been hard on the cat'. Another door led from the workroom onto the verandah and hence outside.

The expeditioners had spent enough time camping outside to find the hut a very cosy place, and on their first night with everybody inside they had the opportunity to judge its blizzard-worthiness. Gale after gale lashed the hut for most of February. Between storms, but still in the face of almost constant strong winds, they erected the radio masts as well as the magnetograph housing (in which only copper nails were supposed to be used) and a hut in which the readings from the magnetographic equipment were recorded. A tide gauge, a snow gauge and other meteorological facilities were built, and an anemometer for measuring wind speeds was firmly attached to a rocky ridge soon known as Anemometer Hill. Such comprehensive surveys had not been attempted before in Antarctica.

Mawson was keen to explore the ice plateau and perhaps establish depots for extended sledging journeys in the spring, but the weather refused to co-operate.

Many of the young men on the expedition had not seen snow before joining the expedition, and at Commonwealth Bay they were to see little else but snow, apart from rocks and the ocean. Percy Correll, the youngest member at age 19, peers over on the lip of an ice cliff.

Where there was snow enough for skis, that's how Mertz travelled. The opportunities were limited and the dangers of not stopping in time fatal. Here Mertz contemplates ice-cliffs at Land's End that drop straight into the ocean.

Mawson was keen to lay depots during the autumn for the sledging journeys he planned for the next summer. However, blizzards and strong winds kept the men trapped in the hut. At last, on 1 March, Mawson was able to lead the first party up the ice-slope south of Cape Denison. Mawson is easy to pick at the front of the sledging team because of his height.

However, an unexpected lull allowed Mawson, with Xavier Mertz and Robert Bage, to put a marker flag three kilometres to the south as part of a plan to establish a line of flags out across the plateau to help sledging parties find their way home in the inevitable blizzards.

With this route-marking project in mind, on 28 February Mawson set out again with Bage and Cecil Madigan, at first with the assistance of Mertz, Bickerton and Hurley. They were able to crest the ice slope nine kilometres from base, at an elevation of 460 metres. This was where they pitched camp, and was to be as far as they got before winter set in, because a blizzard forced them back to the hut the next day. Storms continued to rage – for the month of March the winds averaged 70 kilometres per hour, a 'strong gale' on the Beaufort scale.

During the lead-in to winter, Mawson's team regarded him as a reserved man because he didn't participate in the constant friendly tomfoolery which linked one chore to the next. Some even perceived Mawson as aloof, and he gained the nickname of Dux Ipse, 'the leader himself', often abbreviated to D.I. when they talked among themselves. Mawson's perceived aloofness had less to do with arrogance, nor with regarding himself as a step above his men. Rather, he was preoccupied with the weather. As the only man at Cape Denison with Antarctic experience, Mawson realised, while the others did not, that the conditions they were experiencing here were far worse than those at Ross Island. The rest of the team accepted the conditions at Commonwealth Bay as bleak in the extreme but presumably normal for Antarctica, so they dutifully attended to the tasks they had come here to do, such as the daily checking of the meteorological instruments. In one sense this was very routine work, but the constant blizzards created all sorts of problems, from equipment being blown to pieces or choked with ice to the ink freezing in the recording pens. Several times records were dropped and blown away when the reader was bowled over by a gust of wind.

The magnetic hut had purposely been built several hundred metres from the metal objects in the main hut, so when a blizzard was in full force (which was a large

It may look like the world's most southerly golf course, but the flagpole is the first trail marker erected on the ice slope above Cape Denison. On their first venture inland they were turned back by a blizzard, and Mawson realised the importance of setting up a pole line to help parties find their way back to base when sudden blizzards limited visibility.

On a rare calm day, Percy Correll looks out over Commonwealth Bay and the ice-covered Mackellar Islets from 250 metres above the sea. The dark rocky area of Cape Denison can be seen beyond the crest of the ice slope, with the entrance to Boat Harbour on its left and the icy western shore of the harbour at the left of the picture.

proportion of the time), Eric Webb's daily excursion to collect records for the preceding 24 hours was a serious undertaking indeed. His lot was made even less enviable by the need for regular manual checks of the readings, each of which took four hours to accomplish.

Snow drifted all around the hut, up to its roofline. Eventually it was almost completely covered; ironically, this made it warmer because draughts were kept out. However, it did create a problem when it came to getting in and out of the hut – until a permanent tunnel was dug to a burrow-like exit at a corner which was swept clear by the constant wind. Before the winter was halfway through, Commonwealth Bay was found to be the windiest known place in the world. For a fortnight in May the average wind speed never dropped below 112 kilometres per hour, with the average speed for 14 May being 145 kilometres per hour. The average for the whole month of August was 98 kilometres per hour.

There was plenty of discussion in the hut about the blizzards, and as there were many scientists contributing, they contributed as many theories. It was concluded from observation of clouds travelling at high speeds overhead to the north-north-west, and from the fact that blizzards consistently struck Cape Denison from south-south-east, that they were the victims of a cycling of air. Sixty years before the phrase was invented, they were caught in the ultimate Catch 22. Cold winds swept down from the plateau with enough force to stir up the sea, break any surface ice and prevent sea-ice from forming. This meant that there was exposed water in

Commonwealth Bay year-round. The water was obviously above freezing point, so it warmed, in a relative sense, the very cold air of the blizzard, causing it to rise into the sky, thus creating a vacuum into which the cold air from the plateau now swept. The 'warm' air was dragged across above the plateau, shedding a dozen or more degrees in temperature as it dropped to the surface to fill the void left by the blizzard which was now battering the hut where the scientists sat debating the matter.

In winter the outside temperature was around -33°C, without windchill, so it wasn't surprising that both Cecil Madigan and Alfred Hodgeman were frostbitten when checking the wind speeds at Anemometer Hill. The monitoring of the anemometer was a daily task, for the record sheet had to be changed every 24 hours. One day Hodgeman dropped behind Madigan as they returned to the main hut in the usual blizzard, and he lost his way. He wandered around outside for two hours without moving more than one hundred metres from the hut. When everyone was out looking for him he managed to find his own way back. It was a misadventure he wasn't allowed to forget.

Mawson's reserve hid an anxiety about the ease with which a small mishap such as this could become a disaster, combined with a lingering doubt about the

The space underneath of the hut, accessed via a trapdoor, was used as the expedition's meat freezer. As storeman, Murphy was in charge of fetching the day's meat, but as there was limited room beneath the floor he hit upon the idea of sending a dog through the hatch. Naturally, the dog would emerge with a penguin carcass in its mouth and Murphy would grab the dog and pass its catch onto the cook. On one occasion the dog of the day emerged with one of the expedition's few remaining sides of mutton then managed to squeeze past Murphy with its trophy and dash outside. The chase lasted for over an hour before with the dog was declared the victor. After this event the practice was discontinued.

Despite the constant wind and frequent blizzards, much scientific work was done around Main Base. A tide gauge was set up in a hole dug through the ice of Boat Harbour. Here Bage takes readings of tide levels.

feasibility of post-winter sledging journeys in such a harsh climate. He could only hope that the spring would bring calmer weather. He kept his doubts to himself, and participated in the hut's social life and its daily chores; it was just that laughter didn't come as easily to him at this time as it did to everyone else. However, he wasn't entirely humourless, as his diary shows, noting when one of the tall, heavy-duty radio masts had blown down that the other was likely to follow:

'If it does (fall), it must damage the Hut. Top berths and east side berths at a discount tonight.' On another day he wrote, 'It is quite interesting to stand below the verandah hole exit and watch people looming up through the snow, then disappear as they are blown backwards and again reappear, to vanish as soon. This is repeated often before the haven is reached.'

The chief cause of laughter during the winter was Frank Hurley, who was an incorrigible practical joker. Many of his pranks were very elaborate, and were designed to diffuse the tension which inevitably built up. It was an important contribution to what was, given the very difficult circumstances, a happy winter. Nicknames evolved for most of the men, and with eighteen of them in such a confined space, not even the smallest blunder was missed; instead, they were made into lasting entertainment. Not even Mawson was totally immune. Frank Stillwell and Cecil Madigan revealed no eccentricities and left few openings for being teased. By contrast, a favourite target was Xavier Mertz. X, as he was called, had earned everyone's respect with his display of skiing skills when he conducted classes on a rare windless day in autumn, but his Swiss accent and misuse of Australian idiom was a constant source of mirth. Ninnis received many taunts for misreading a recipe and adding two ounces of both salt and pepper to a baked dish which looked and smelt and delicious when it came out of the oven but was totally inedible. Meals were the high points of the day, and great care had to be taken in cooking them if a man were to retain his self-respect. But entertainment was not always at someone else's expense. When there was still daylight, favourite sports were being blown across the nearby frozen lake and tobogganing down slopes on boards. Herbert Murphy was a great spinner of yarns, and there were many books to read. There was a gramophone, and once during the winter, a not-so-grand opera was written, rehearsed and presented in the hut.

Simple chores such as reading the tide gauge became hazardous in blizzards. It was possible to get blown along the sea-ice and into the ocean, but luckily this never happened. When the winds were at their strongest everyone stayed inside, but for people caught out when the wind speed picked up to hurricane force the only way to get back to the hut against the wind was to crawl along using an ice-axe.

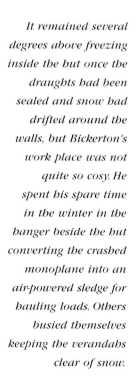

Frank Hurley always found a way to entertain himself, such as arranging this photograph of him trimming Hunter's beard.

There was also plenty of work to do, from hut chores and equipment repairs to the ongoing scientific projects. When the radio masts were finally erected securely, Hannam and Bickerton were kept busy sending messages, although they received no replies. They had no way of knowing that several of their messages were successfully transmitted to Macquarie Island station, thus becoming the first-ever radio contact from Antarctica.

Although Mawson had his worries, he was fascinated by the situation they found themselves in. 'How can any whole-minded being be dull here?' he wrote in his diary. 'Even though cooped up in the Hut by blizzard upon blizzard? How can anyone, when there is so much unknown about us?'

He also considered possibilities. He recorded his experiment with melting blubber for oil, then he calculated the Commonwealth Bay area's commercial potential from seal and penguin oil products. Given the ferocity of the climate, it would have made more sense for him to re-examine the feasibility of his father's entrepreneurial projects in tropical New Guinea.

It remained several degrees above freezing inside the hut once the draughts had been sealed and snow had drifted around the walls, but Bickerton's work place was not quite so cosy. He spent his spare time in the winter in the hanger beside the hut converting the crashed monoplane into an air-powered sledge for hauling loads. Others busied themselves keeping the verandahs clear of snow.

By the time winter set in, the Main Base hut was buried by drift snow up to the roof line. To the north of the hut is the flat sea ice which covers two-thirds of Boat Harbour. The tide gauge can be seen towards the left of the sea-ice.

A winter afternoon in the hut shows some of the men relaxing in the hut. Mertz on the left is reading, Hunter uses the microscope, Madigan is busy on the table, another man dozing hides a fifth man in the background. The photo also shows the library and how every available space is used for storage. Not shown is the constant howl of the blizzard and the barking of the dogs as they squabble in the snow tunnel leading off the verandah.

One night he went out into the blizzard specifically to 'enquire after the St Elmo's fire', (atmospheric electric corona discharge). He wandered around outside comparing the discharge of sparks when he was standing on rock, on ice and on the roof of the hut. He noted that 'it sparks better on sharpened copper wire than on an ice axe'. On the same excursion he found that 'one can roll up quite happily in the blizzard in a small lee after closing the burberry funnel (the hood of his burberry jacket). This is valuable in case one should get lost in a blizzard.'

Mawson led by example, not as a strategy to influence his men but because he was the kind of man who always made sure the job got done. In the process he had his own misadventures, courtesy of the blizzards. Once he lost his bearings outside in a storm for a short time, and another day when fetching blocks of ice to be melted for water, 'I was carried off my feet completely on one occasion whilst carrying a block in a stooping position'.

During the winter, preparations were made for sledging journeys in the spring. Of course, Mawson was completely unfamiliar with what lay inland from Commonwealth Bay, and he also knew almost nothing about the 500 kilometres of coastline *Aurora* had skirted to get to Cape Denison because bad weather and

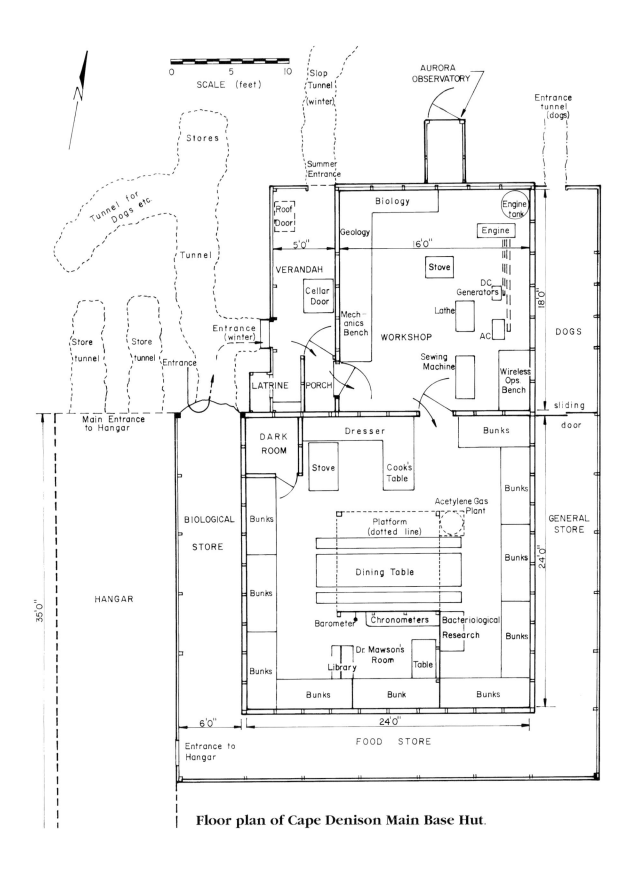

Floor plan of Cape Denison Main Base Hut.

pack-ice had kept it either out of sight or beyond the southern horizon. With his thirst for discovery it was frustrating in the extreme to be so pinned down by the weather. A year spent at Cape Denison would certainly provide data about the windiest place in the world, which would be a valuable addition to knowledge of Antarctica's climate, but with a team of 18 strong and committed expeditioners Mawson was keen to explore as much of this unknown land as he could. He formed plans for six sledging parties, but reconnaissances and the laying of supply depots had to be done first. He also developed a strategy to help deal with the constant blizzards, namely the digging of ice caves to provide safe haven in the worst of storms.

By August the Antarctic winter was drawing to an end. At the first opportunity Mawson sledged south with Madigan, Ninnis and Mertz and eight dogs, taking a load of provisions to their depot nine kilo-

Snow drifted into the open-ended verandahs of the hut so that tunnels, known as the catacombs, had to be dug in order to get outside. There was a tunnel for the dogs, another for slops from the kitchen, and several for stores.

metres away. Here they dug an ice cave to provide a sledging base that would not be destroyed by winds. Mawson named it Aladdin's Cave, and jotted in his diary, 'a truly magical cave for in it perfect peace whilst outside a roaring blizzard'. One of its advantages was a narrow but apparently bottomless crevasse in one corner which could be used for waste disposal, including human – a great convenience when the weather was foul outside. They pushed on for five more kilometres and established another depot before heading for home, where Mawson learnt that in their absence the wind hadn't blown as strongly at the hut as it had up on the plateau. The sledging journeys would be serious undertakings indeed, particularly as the strong winds had stopped sea-ice forming along the base of the ice cliffs. Solid sea-ice provided crevasse-free, level terrain for sledging but here all journeys would have to start on the plateau beyond Aladdin's Cave. Several journeys were made to the cave with supplies, including some using Bickerton's now functional air tractor.

In September, three reconnaissance journeys took place. Mawson wanted to give everyone a taste of sledging before they undertook their major journeys. Certainly

Hunter (left), Hodgeman and Bage wash up after dinner at Winter Quarters, Cape Denison. Those on washing up duty always expressed great interest in the cook's proposed menu, not out of hunger but because they wanted to know how much fat was to be used in the recipes. Washing up in water that was never very hot to begin with and always cooled quickly was a chore made much worse by greasy dishes.

The photographer does not seem to have captured a happy moment at this Midwinter dinner, 1912. Nevertheless, it was a special day, and was celebrated as such, as it signified the passing of the expedition's 'darkest hours', in a literal sense. Mawson wears a dark coat in the centre of the back row, Mertz in front centre with dark moustache and Ninnis is second from Mawson's right.

all members soon experienced the hazards of camping in Antarctic blizzards. In their first two-week excursion, Madigan, Whetter and Close laid a depot 80 kilometres from Main Base but had their tent torn apart by a storm as they struggled to return. Ninnis, Mertz and Murphy had to turn around 30 kilometres south-east of Main Base when their tent was similarly destroyed. A blizzard hit Webb, McLean and Stillwell as they finished digging a second ice cave 19 kilometres south of Main Base. After three days of relative comfort in the cave, which they named The Cathedral Grotto, the blizzard eased sufficiently for them to head home.

The weather remained bad, but the arrival of Adelie penguins in mid-October was a definite sign that summer, and the penguin breeding season, were on their way. It wasn't until early November that the five sledging parties were able set out on their major journeys. The Southern Party, with its destination the South Magnetic Pole, consisted of Robert Bage as leader with Eric Webb as magnetician, and the

With the arrival of spring, everyone was keen to explore beyond the range of the meteorological and other scientific instruments, which had been the limits of their excursions during the bleakest months. Here a figure crosses a steep snow slope above sea-ice that has not frozen solid even after winter. A fall from here would be very dangerous as he would most likely drop over the ice-cliff, break through the ice below and sink without a trace.

After his experience with the slowness of sledge-hauling over the sticky surface of sea-ice during his journey to the South Magnetic Pole in 1908–09, Mawson designed this sledge with removable wheels, which worked well enough. However, the extraordinarily strong winds at Cape Denison prevented sea-ice forming to the strength suitable for extended sea-ice journeys. Nor were short journeys attempted because the unbroken ice-cliffs to the east and west of Cape Denison allowed no emergency escape routes should the sea-ice start to break while sledging parties were on it.

Bickerton's many hours of labour converting the crashed aeroplane into a air-powered sledge paid off. Here he tries the propellor. The air-tractor provided a novel form of transport across the sea-ice of Boat Harbour, before ferrying loads up to Aladdin's Cave.

irrepressible Frank Hurley. They faced a journey of 550 kilometres to the Magnetic Pole. In order to hasten their progress, they were supported by Herbert Murphy, 'Joe' Laseron and Johnnie Hunter.

The support party returned to the hut by the end of November, whereupon Laseron joined Frank Stillwell (leader), and John Close to form the Near East Coast Party, which mapped the coastline to the Mertz Glacier. By the time Stillwell's team left base, the Eastern Coastal Party of 'Dad' McLean, Percy Correll and Cecil Madigan (leader), were well on their way to mapping the terrain east of the country slated for Stillwell's party. Madigan and his team were able to drop onto sea-ice near the Mertz Glacier. They made good progress on that level surface until slowed down by the Ninnis Glacier Tongue. However, perhaps because of inexperience, they pushed themselves almost too far, allowing no latitude for bad weather or worsening snow conditions, both of which they encountered on the return journey. Madigan made a ten-hour solo push to one of their depots and brought back enough food for them to sit out the ensuing three-day blizzard and regain the strength to haul their sledge back to Main Base.

Members of the Eastern Sledge Journey were delighted to encounter several dramatic rock formations because they provided relief from the endless blues and whites of the ice and snow they travelled across for weeks on end. Cecil Madigan was particularly pleased, as he was a geologist who later worked with Mawson at the University of Adelaide. Here Madigan climbs the sandstone formation of Horn Bluff, 330 kilometres east-southeast of Main Base.

Also at the beginning of November the Western Party of Frank Bickerton, Leslie Whetter and Alfred Hodgeman left Base with the air tractor carrying their supplies and equipment. Perhaps its load of 500 kilograms was too great in the cold conditions, because on the second day the engine seized, so it was sledge-hauling from there onwards for this team as well. They man-hauled 250 kilometres from Base, and of this distance 156 kilometres were covered in a remarkable five-day spell of good weather. They reached their most westerly point on Christmas Day, and returned to Main Base only three days after Mawson's 15 January deadline.

The other parties had made it back to Cape Denison before the deadline, apart from the one which had been last to leave – the Far Eastern Party, under the command of Mawson himself.

The Southern Support Party of Hunter (left), Murphy and Laseron on 22 November 1912, about to head back to Main Base after establishing the Southern Cross Depot – which the South Magnetic Pole Party was unable to locate on their return.

CHAPTER 6

Dux Ipse

This shot of Mertz on an earlier stage of the journey shows the effectiveness of the burberry hood in keeping out snow. During the sledging journeys clothing and equipment was constantly being damaged and repaired, as the patched elbow of Mertz's burberry jacket demonstrates.

As its name suggests, the goal of the Far Eastern Party was to explore the coast further to the east than the region assigned to McLean and his Eastern Party. To reach this distant coast Mawson decided to use two dog teams of eight dogs each. His companions for the journey would be Mertz and Ninnis, who had been engaged as dog-handlers when Mawson had been in England, where he had also obtained the expedition's team of Greenland dogs. Neither Ninnis nor Mertz had had any experience with handling such dogs before the expedition, but they'd looked after them during the winter and learnt to sledge with them in the spring. Mawson trusted their judgement, but as he himself hadn't travelled with dogs before the expedition, he was understandably concerned about how well they would perform on the ambitious journey he had planned. Having been unable to land a wintering party to the east of Cape Denison, he wished to push as far as he could in that direction with the dogs.

In early November, Mawson was distracted by the need to make sure everything was in order with the other sledging parties, so the final preparations for his own team were given less attention. Despite the excitement and momentum of the departures, Mawson found time to write a last-minute letter to Paquita.

'I am writing this note in case anything may happen which will prevent me reaching you... So many things may intervene for one truly lives but from day to day here and then our sledge journey is about to commence... It is unlikely any harm will happen to us but should I not return to you in Australia please know that I truly loved you.'

Mawson, Ninnis and Mertz left Main Base two days after the others, on 10 November. The dogs proved themselves on the first day and they caught up with the southbound and eastbound man-hauling teams at Aladdin's Cave. Although they had time and energy to continue, Mawson decided to spend their first night in the cave because he wanted to check supplies and leave instructions for Murphy, who was ahead leading the Southern Party's support team.

The three teams leapfrogged from lunch to campsite for the next day and a half, then after a final lunch together and much shaking of hands, Mawson and his team pushed ahead, with the dogs pulling strongly. 'The pace, if anything, was too rapid,' wrote Mawson, 'for capsizes were apt to occur in racing over high sastrugi. Any doubts as to the capability of the dogs to pull the loads were dispelled.'

After the desperately hard work of hauling sledges with Edgeworth David and Mackay during the British Antarctic Expedition, Mawson was delighted to have their

After the long winter which kept the men trapped in the hut and the dogs restricted to the tunnels dug in the snow-clogged verandah, everyone was looking forward to some time spent outside. Here Ninnis and Mertz, who had become firm friends on the voyage out from England, harness the dogs at Main Base in preparation for their long journey inland.

loads whisked along by the dogs. In ideal conditions they covered 30 kilometres a day, although sometimes difficult and dangerous terrain lessened their progress dramatically. And, as expected, they spent days at a time holed up in the tent while blizzards blasted their camp. In the fiercest storms Mawson took the precaution of putting all his belongings in a single bag in case the tent did tear apart. Despite the climate, the other aspects of life continued, with Gagdet, a pregnant bitch, travelling on the sledge and then having pups.

As well as contending with storms, they had to navigate crevasse fields. The big, gaping crevasses could be skirted but hidden ones were harder to avoid. Temporary but painful snow blindness also became a problem, caused by staring into the glare for danger signs. One afternoon, as they were pulling down their tent after eating lunch inside it, Ninnis stepped back and broke through the snow into a crevasse. Luckily, he caught himself on the lip before he disappeared from sight. He dragged himself out onto the snow, and when they peered into the hole he'd made, they saw that they'd pitched their tent on top of a five metre-wide crevasse. They stared down into the blackness of this perfect example of the danger posed by crevasses. A firm crust of snow had formed on the surface, hiding the fact that in the glacier's gradual slide down towards the distant sea, the ice had cracked apart beneath the crust, creating huge hidden crevasses.

After this incident they took even more care. As they progressed further east, they reached terrain where the crevasses were easier to avoid because there was no sur-face crust. In places they had to find a way though a maze of crevasses, formed when the ice was contorted by a slight ridge or some other obstacle hidden deep below the surface of the glacier. Low clouds and swirling snow made navigation difficult, but at least the clouds trapped what little heat there was in the sun. In such conditions daytime temperatures were occasionally above freezing, which was enough to make the snow stick to the sledge runners, slowing the team down. Often their course lay across vast expanses of sastrugi; progress was slowed considerably as they battled their way across these wind-carved ridges of ice.

Disaster was narrowly averted when Mawson's dogs, pulling two sledges, crossed a snow bridge across a gaping crevasse then changed direction – before the second sledge was on the snow bridge. Consequently, the second sledge missed the snow bridge altogether and plunged into the crevasse, dragging the first sledge and the dogs backwards. Mawson struggled to stop the backwards slide, managing to hold onto the front sledge long enough for Ninnis and Mertz to drive ice-axes behind the sledge runners and then anchor the sledge in place with a rope. Extracting the sledge was quite a process, with the most exciting part being when Mawson was lowered into the crevasse by Ninnis and Mertz so he could attach a rope to the rear of the sledge. Afterwards Mawson noted with satisfaction, 'No more remarkable test of the efficiency of the sledge straps and the compactness of the load could have been made.' The incident also taught them all the importance of paying close attention to the path taken not only by the dogs, but also by the sledges.

By 12 December, they had covered 480 kilometres from Main Base; they'd driven themselves and their dogs hard to do so. One of their three sledges was severely damaged, and as they had consumed a month's worth of fuel and food for both themselves and the dogs, they were able to cache the broken sledge and and a small amount of spare equipment. They repacked the loads onto the two remaining ones and travelled much better with this revised set-up. Their spirits were high – they'd had good views of the coast in recent days, had named a prominent peninsula Cape Freshfield, and were thinking of establishing a depot, then making a final lightweight dash to the east before turning for home.

Early in the afternoon on 14 December, Mertz was ahead on skis scouting the route, with Mawson 300 metres behind walking beside the leading sledge. He noticed Mertz raise his ski stock as a signal. As Mertz then continued skiing, Mawson could see no reason for the warning, so he hopped onto his sledge to compute the latitude from readings he had taken at noon. The dogs were still pulling the sledge as he scribbled in his notebook, and he noticed a slight dip pass beneath the runners of the sledge. This must have been the concealed crevasse Mertz had spotted. Mawson had now crossed it without incident, but he took the precaution of calling back to Ninnis, only ten metres behind him, who then steered his dogs squarely across the slight depression in order to take a shorter course across the possible danger zone. This was routine practice, and Mawson would have done the same had he noticed the depression before he was on top of it.

Mawson returned to his calculations. He heard the whimper of a dog but assumed it was Ninnis making use of his whip and thought nothing of it. He glanced up a minute later to see that he was drawing closer to Mertz, who had stopped and was looking back. Mawson, too, turned round and was amazed to see no sign of

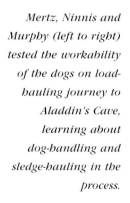

Mertz, Ninnis and Murphy (left to right) tested the workability of the dogs on load-hauling journey to Aladdin's Cave, learning about dog-handling and sledge-hauling in the process.

Ninnis and Mertz urge the dogs onwards at jogging pace on easy terrain. In good conditions, up to 30 kilometres were covered in a day. Amundsen was to cover much greater distances but in better conditions. Distances were measured with a sledge-meter constructed from a bicycle wheel with a revolution counter attached; one can be seen at the rear of the sledge.

Ninnis. Remembering the crevasse, he jumped off the sledge and ran back, hoping that Ninnis was hidden by a dip in the snow. But of course they were no such dips. He found instead a gaping hole, with two sets of sledge tracks leading to it. Only Mawson's tracks continued on the other side. Mawson shouted, but no reply came. Ninnis, his sledge and his dogs had vanished, it seemed, without a trace. Mertz hurriedly skied back, and when he and Mawson peered over the edge they saw two dogs on a ledge which protruded from one wall far below. One dog was dead and the other appeared to have broken its back. Apart from some wreckage next to them, there was no sign of anything else. With a fishing line they measured that the distance to the ledge – it was 45 metres down, well beyond the length of their alpine rope. The crevasse was several metres wide and sheer walls of featureless ice dropped vertically into blackness.

'At such moments action is the only tolerable thing,' wrote Mawson, but there was absolutely nothing they could do. They called and listened and called again, hour after hour. Time was blurred by the power of the tragedy. At last they accepted the obvious, awful truth that Ninnis was gone. They stood by the side of the crevasse as Mawson read the Burial Service.

The disaster was worse than the loss of their friend, 'my best friend in the entire expedition', as Mertz wrote in his diary that night. Ninnis' sledge had the best dogs and most of their essential equipment. They had planned it this way, expecting that the sledge in front would be the one to break through into a hidden crevasse, as this had happened to them many times already. But none of these encounters had been with a crevasse anywhere near as large as this one. Mertz on skis had passed over it safely, as had Mawson sitting on his sledge. In both these cases, weight was distributed along skis or sledge runners one and a half metres or more in length. Ninnis, however, had been walking beside his sledge, and the pressure of one foot had obviously been greater than Mawson's runners or Mertz's skis. Ninnis had punched a hole in the crust, whereupon the lid of the crevasse gave way, plummeting him, then the sledge and the dogs to their doom.

The finger of blame has been pointed at Mawson for not encouraging his expeditioners to use the skis that he'd brought out from England, but this is the 'wisdom' of hindsight. None of the other expeditioners suffered any penalty for not using skis. Mawson had decided that the winds were so strong in this region that skis were too dangerous for everyone except Mertz, an acknowledged expert. As Mertz noted in his diary on the day of the disaster, it happened at 'a crevasse like hundreds we have crossed in the last weeks.' On this day, Mawson had been the man at greatest risk, as he was with the leading sledge. Every day they had battled obvious dangers and taken precautions against the ones they couldn't see. But in this case Fate got the better of them.

Along with Ninnis in the depths of the crevasse lay what had been the strongest dogs, their tent, their shovel and almost all the food for themselves and the dogs. As it had been such a fine day, Mertz had also left his burberry overtrousers with Ninnis, an act which was to cost him dearly. Mawson's leading sledge carried their sleeping bags, ten days' worth of food and their personal kit. They also had a stove and kerosene, without which they would have quickly died of thirst. Back at their abandoned sled they had a tent cover but not the floor or the poles, so they had to make this small cache their destination for that night.

Nine hours after the accident, immediately after reading the Burial Service, they turned for home. Mawson decided not to go north to the coast, where they may have been able to live off the land as he had done during the B.A.E., because all he had seen of that rugged coastline suggested that it would be impossible for the ship to collect them from there – if it even occurred to Captain Davis to try. As Mawson saw it, their only hope lay in eating the dogs, although with them they had only the

Mawson leans against the ice-axes on the sledge without apparent discomfort during a rest on the way to Aladdin's Cave. It was the first day out of Main Base on his long journey to the east with Ninnis and Mertz.

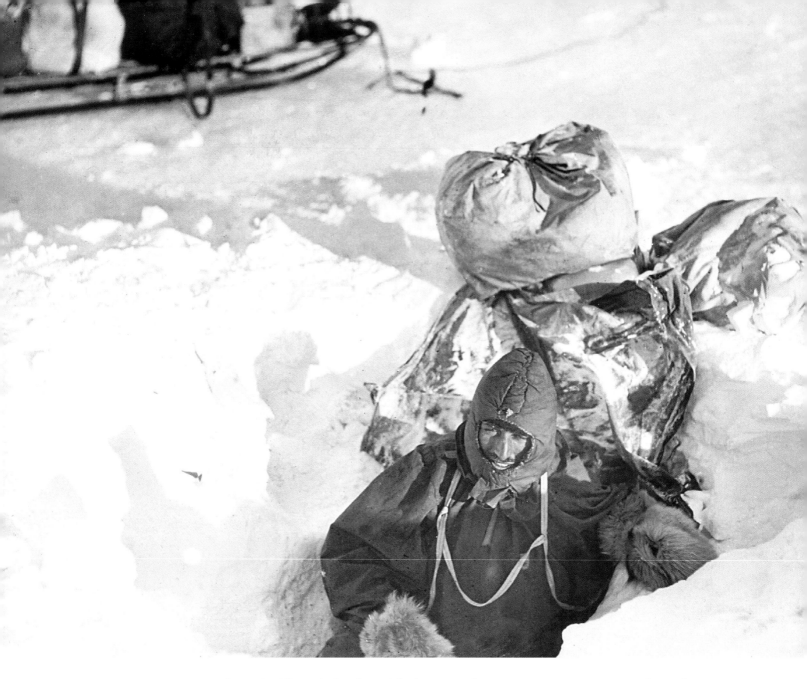

With a loaded sledge ready to go, Mertz emerges from the entry tunnel to Aladdin's Cave. Behind him is the canvas flap used to keep snow out of the entrance.

weakest six. They sledged at night because daytime temperatures were above freezing and made the snow too soft. They paused at their abandoned sledge to fashion some spoons and makeshift tent poles. They also picked up the tent cover and a shovel, which was a very important tool in a place where the sledge was frequently buried by a storm or drifting snow. Both men pulled with dogs, then they killed one of the dogs and fed it to the others, which gave them the strength to pull without Mawson and Mertz. But it was desperately slow going, and navigation was difficult because the sky was heavily overcast. In the dull whiteness it was impossible to see detail in the surface of the snow. Both men constantly tripped over sastrugi, weakening themselves even further. On 21 December, the clouds lifted briefly and they spotted their first familiar landmark. 'Dixon Island stood out in the north for a moment,' wrote Mawson, 'miraged above the horizon. We felt we had met an old friend, which means a lot in that icy desolation.' Then a strong wind blasted them with drifting snow, and the reassuring image was gone.

On 23 December they killed Pavlova, the second last of their dogs, and Mawson began to talk of making soup out of their finnesko boots. Their remaining dog, Ginger, no longer had the strength to pull. Nor did the men, on meagre rations and the stewed meat of starved dogs, but they made themselves do it. They were 180 kilometres from the site of the tragedy, with 300 kilometres ahead of them. That night they cooked their supply of dog meat, then ate a soup made of bones. They lightened the loads on their sledges as much as they could, but the next day, as they struggled uphill in soft snow, they ditched more in desperation, including their camera and film, spare clothing, and their instrument box – but not the instruments, as it was with these that they must find their way.

On Christmas Day they vowed to compensate for this year's austerity with the most glorious Christmas dinners imaginable in the future. For now they acknowledged the day with a little butter on their dog meat.

'I hope to have many happy Christmasses yet with my friend Mawson,' wrote Mertz. But by 30 December he fell ill, on top of the constant state of exhaustion. Mawson did everything he could to keep Mertz's spirits up because he knew that this was vital if Mertz was to survive. During this time 'it was agreed that once on board the ship, Mertz was to spend the day making penguin egg omelettes, for the excellence of those he had made prior to leaving the hut had not been forgotten.' But as the days passed, Mertz became weaker and weaker, until Mawson hauled him on the sledge, knowing that if they stopped making progress every day they would be accepting death. By 7 January, Mawson had to help Mertz into his sleeping bag because he longer had the strength to do it himself. He lost control of his bowels, so Mawson cleaned his trousers and put them back on him as Mertz could no longer do this himself. As his companion lay in his sleeping bag, Mawson wrote in his diary, feeling that the end was near for both of them.

'I don't mind for myself, but it is for Paquita and for all others connected with the expedition that I feel so deeply and sinfully. I pray for God to help us.'

He roused Mertz with some thick cocoa and beef tea, but he had to hold him up so he could drink it. Mertz fouled his pants again and Mawson cleaned them again. Soon he became delirious, talking incoherently and struggling against Mawson's efforts to keep him in his sleeping bag. At midnight he became peaceful and

This snapshot taken by Archie McLean shows Mawson, Ninnis and Mertz heading away from the Aladdin's Cave on 11 November 1912. It is the last photograph of the trio that has survived, as on his lone journey back to Main Base Mawson jettisoned everything he could to reduce the weight he had to haul behind him, and this included all cameras and all films.

Mawson clambered into his own bag to warm himself. Two hours later Mawson stretched out his arm and felt that his friend was stiff in death. 'All that remained was his mortal frame which, toggled up in his sleeping bag, still offered some sense of companionship as I threw myself down for the remainder of the night, revolving in my mind all that lay behind and the chances of the future.'

In the morning, Mawson buried Mertz under a pile of snow blocks, then he cut the sledge in half and made a rough cross out of the runners of the discarded part. For the second time in a month he read the Burial Service, no doubt thinking that there would be no-one to read his own. He had known from the moment they'd turned their backs on Ninnis' grave that every day of the homeward journey must count if they were to have any chance of survival. Mertz's gradual demise had cost precious time they could not afford, but he had seen no alternative to keeping them moving inexorably homewards, no matter how slowly. Now the struggle would be to keep himself moving. He knew that his body, too, was falling apart. He was losing skin from his legs and genitals, and the sores on his hands wouldn't heal.

Debate continues about whether the two men gave themselves Vitamin A poisoning by eating dog livers. The extraordinary nutritional requirements of

130

sledge-hauling in extreme cold were not at all understood in those days, and both men demanded more of their bodies than their bodies had to give. In these impossible circumstances it was the body of Mertz, and perhaps his willpower, that gave out first, whether poisoned or just severely malnourished.

With his half-sledge and pruned-back equipment, Mawson headed north-west. It seems from his diaries that at first he held little hope of surviving, but was determined to reach a landmark, perhaps Aurora Peak, where his and Mertz's diaries and the records of the 480 kilometres the three of them had surveyed might be found by a search party. But his resolve quickly returned to give him everything in his power to make it back to Main Base. Of course he knew that it might well be an impossible task, but he also knew that he would have no chance at all if he showed the slightest weakness of will. And there is no doubt that he found extra strength in the responsibilities he felt to the expedition and to Paquita. They gave him a focus, and a motivation, beyond himself.

His first obstacle was the tortured terrain of the Mertz Glacier. Many of its countless crevasses were hidden, and there were slopes of hard ice and depressions filled with soft snow. He struggled forwards on starvation rations, and at every meal he battled the temptation to double or triple the amount he was allowing himself.

Mawson navigated on the Far Eastern Sledge Journey by taking observations of the sun, and also by setting a course according to the sastrugi, as these ridges of ice were always aligned to the direction of the prevailing wind. Some distance to the north of Mawson's team, a member of the Eastern Party takes a sun observation for latitude.

There were many signs that his body was giving up the struggle. 'Saliva glands of mouth refusing duty, skin coming off whole body,' he records matter-of-factly. One evening when he took his socks off, he was horrified to see that the soles of his feet came off with them. He put his soles back where they belonged and he tied them back in place.

All the sledging parties encountered blizzards, which either swept snow from the surface and exposed slippery ice, or covered everything with deep snow, such as at this camp of the furthest-west sledging team.

On 17 January he pushed on despite very poor visibility, with 'Providence' guiding him between gaping crevasses. Deep snow frustrated him as he stumbled onwards, then suddenly he broke through into a hidden crevasse. He dangled there at the end of his sledge harness, then slowly began to drop as the sledge crept towards the lip of the crevasse. He expected the sledge to crash in on top of him, thus ending the story, but then slowly everything stopped moving. He was hanging in air several metres below the surface in a smooth-walled crevasse two metres wide.

'Above at the other end of the 14-foot rope was the daylight seen through the hole in the lid. In my weak condition, the prospect of climbing out seemed very poor indeed. A great effort brought a knot in the rope within grasp, and after a moment's rest, I was able to draw myself up and reach another, and, at length, hauled my body onto the overhanging snow lid. Then, when all appeared well and before I could quite get to solid ground, a further section of the lid gave way, precipitating me once more to the full length of the rope.'

The effort had exhausted him and it seemed there was no way out. His immediate thought was one of anger at not having eaten the remaining food on the sledge. He felt hunger for that food, and then for life, and so he hauled himself, hand over hand, up the rope, only to fall back from the lip.

'I felt I had done my utmost and failed, that I had no more strength to try again and that all was over except the passing. It was to be a miserable and slow end... but

This crevasse was exposed when the photographer broke through the frozen snow crust. All parties faced this hazard, but as all sledging teams had at least three men, the victim was quickly hauled to the surface. Alone and weakened, Mawson invented his own system of crevasse rescue — an improvised rope ladder.

there always remained the alternative of slipping from the harness (and plunging into the depths of the crevasse). From those flights of mind I came back to earth and remembering how Providence had miraculously brought me so far, felt nothing was impossible... Fired by the passion that burns in the act of strife, new power seemed to come as I applied myself to one last tremendous effort.'

On the third attempt he hauled himself out onto the snow, where he lay motionless for an indeterminate time until until he could muster the energy to pitch his improvised tent.

Mawson had accepted that he would die when in the crevasse, and yet here he was in his sleeping bag, getting warm. There was life in him yet, but how much, he didn't know. Should he eat all his food now, he wondered, to avoid the anger at not having done so the next time he fell in to a crevasse? He knew he wouldn't have the strength to climb out again as he had done that day. He considered his options

– admittedly few – then felt strengthened by a plan. He ate only his allotted ration. The following morning before striking camp he spent several hours making a rope ladder which he attached to the sledge and hooked over his shoulder, ready for his next plunge into icy space. The next day he found that the system worked well, although every crevasse he fell into weakened him further.

There has been much speculation about what enabled Mawson to survive. His response to near-death in the crevasse gives a good clue. Mawson was undoubtedly tough in every sense of the word, which certainly helped, but it was the way that his mind constantly reassessed the problems ahead of him that allowed him to keep pushing on. He learnt from every mishap, then implemented his revised plan or technique. He changed his immediate goals, and in this way prevented the enormity of the obstacles ahead overwhelming him. He never relied totally on Providence because he didn't see Providence in those terms. He felt Providence as a definite yet

In Mawson's archives, this photo by Frank Hurley bears the caption 'Improvised tent used by Dr. Mawson on his fateful journey'. However, Hurley had left Cape Denison by the time Mawson returned to Main Base alone and without a camera. It is likely that Hurley set up the photo when he returned to Cape Denison as part of the rescue mission in December 1913. Hurley was a very talented and imaginative photographer, who went to great lengths to obtain the images he desired, and he certainly appreciated that Mawson's solo journey was an important part of the story that would need illustrating in lecture tours, newspapers and the expedition book, Home of the Blizzard.

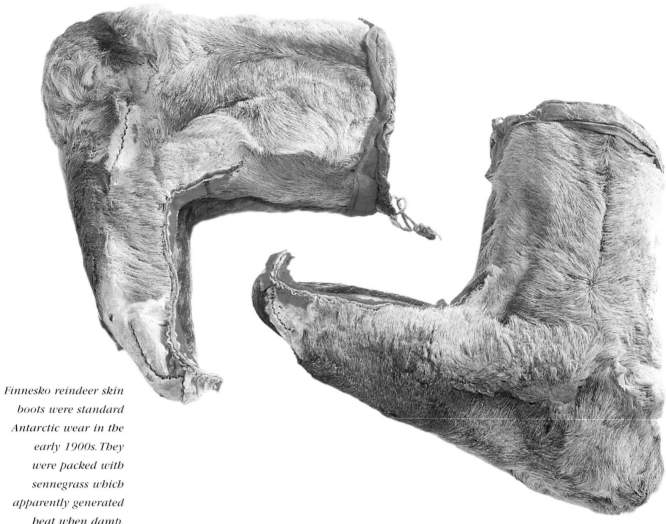

Finnesko reindeer skin boots were standard Antarctic wear in the early 1900s. They were packed with sennegrass which apparently generated heat when damp. Every night the grass was dried out and the boots packed with fresh grass to maintain their shape. If this wasn't done, the boots froze flat and it was impossible to get a foot in. After Ninnis died and rations were low, Mawson discussed with Mertz the possibility of making soup out of their finneskos.

indefinable presence, not something supernatural, not something which gave him power or the promise of salvation, but a watchful, silent, somehow reassuring reminder of the absolute necessity of making sure that every step was followed by another.

After struggling through the heavily crevassed area for several days, re-testing his ladder as he went, he decided to increase his rations. Although much of this was dog meat from dogs killed at the point of exhaustion, it gave Mawson extra strength. On 29 January, he calculated that Aladdin's Cave must be less than 50 kilometres distant. The windblown snow which continued into the next day made navigation difficult, making it even more remarkable that he noticed a cairn 300 metres to his north. He diverted to what turned out to be a snow mound draped with a black cloth for extra visibility. He was stunned to find a note from McLean, Hodgeman and

Hurley, who had left that morning, having camped within a few kilometres of Mawson. They probably would have been within sight of each other had snow not been blowing across the landscape. The note gave a bearing to Aladdin's Cave, 34 kilometres away, as well as the news that the ship had arrived and that the other sledging parties were safe. It was six weeks since Ninnis' death, and for almost half of this time Mawson had been alone. It is likely that Mawson thanked Providence again, on several counts.

His epic was not over yet, though, and he knew it. He was delighted to have real food again, but was also wary of loading his sledge with too much weight to pull in his weakened condition. It took him two more days to reach Aladdin's Cave. His progress was hampered by the fact that he'd thrown away his crampons, which meant he was constantly blown over on the slippery ice on the crest of the plateau. Once at the cave, he was startled to discover a pineapple. The ship certainly had arrived. There was plenty of food for him now, and he had plenty of time to improvise new crampons, as well as a spare pair, because a blizzard blew in for five days.

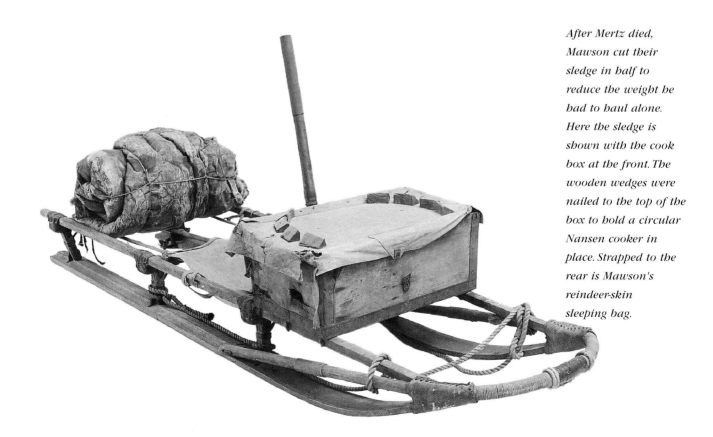

After Mertz died, Mawson cut their sledge in half to reduce the weight he had to haul alone. Here the sledge is shown with the cook box at the front. The wooden wedges were nailed to the top of the box to hold a circular Nansen cooker in place. Strapped to the rear is Mawson's reindeer-skin sleeping bag.

When Ninnis suddenly vanished into a crevasse along with his dogs and sledge, Mawson and Mertz lost not only their companion but also most of their food, the strongest teams of dogs, and important equipment, including spoons, so Mawson and Mertz made their own. Mawson navigated the 480 kilometres back to Cape Denison using this theodolite. He protected himself from the glare and blinding snow of blizzards with the goggles shown. As he approached the crest of the ice-plateau above Cape Denison, the wind and sun exposed had a vast area of hard blue ice. Unfortunately, to save weight Mawson had previously discarded his Swiss-made mountaineering crampons which would have allowed him to walk on the ice, and so he had to improvise the ones shown here out of boards, nails and leather straps.

It was typical of Cape Denison, but it was not Mawson's choice of welcome.

He also had time to improvise rope brakes for the sledge runners to prevent the sledge careening away from him on the downhill run to Main Base. He also added a 'patent anti-crevasse bar', presumably some kind of pole which would span any crevasse that the sledge might slide into. A lesser man may have taken the risk of attempting the final 12 kilometres of the 960-kilometre round trip without the security of a sledge carrying a stove, food and shelter, but Mawson had come this far, pushing every limit but still taking every precaution. At this point he had no strength left to take chances, and he was determined not to perish in a sudden blizzard within sight of Main Base.

On 8 February, when the winds eased early in the afternoon, he let gravity take him down the long ice slope towards Cape Denison. As he descended out of swirling snow he could see no sign of the ship in Commonwealth Bay, except perhaps the smallest black line on the horizon. But as Boat Harbour came into view, he saw some men working there, and his spirits rose. He waved, and they spotted

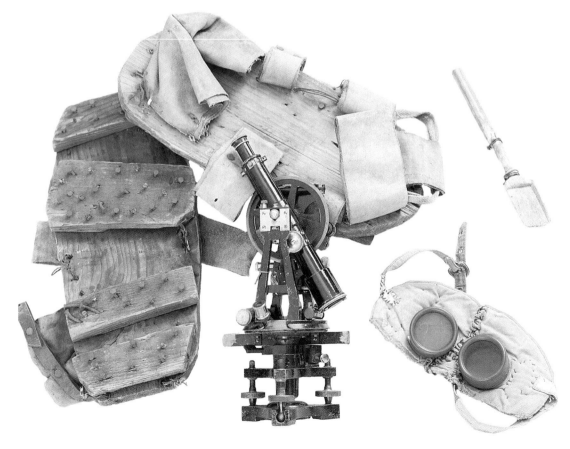

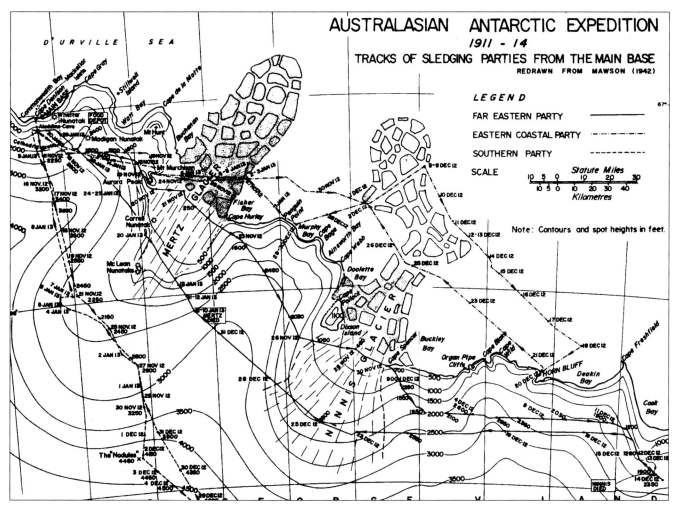

LEGEND

FAR EASTERN PARTY ————————

EASTERN COASTAL PARTY ·—·—·—·—

SOUTHERN PARTY ————————

SCALE

Note: Contours and spot heights in feet.

him almost immediately. Five men rushed up the hill towards him. Bickerton reached him first, then Bage, McLean, Madigan and Hodgeman as a group. None could at first tell which of the three missing men he was. Their delight at seeing their leader again turned to horror as Mawson told them, in a few brief words at first, that Ninnis and Mertz were dead.

Map of King George Land, prepared by Mawson for use in the scientific report in 1942. This map is based on the version modified for the Jacka's edited Mawson's Antarctic Diaries *in 1988. It shows the tracks of some of the sledging parties from the Main Base. The cartographer there was A.J. Hodgman, who was acknowledged by Mawson in* The Home of the Blizzard *for drawing up the maps used by Mawson in 1914.*

CHAPTER 7

Cold Comfort

The entire coastline explored by the A.A.E. was effectively unchartered, as much of the information available to Captain Davis from earlier voyages proved inaccurate. The presence of low rocky islands, named the Mackellar Islets, off Cape Denison, signalled dangerous waters, so when Davis returned to Commonwealth Bay in January 1914, he anchored Aurora *one nautical mile offshore (1.8 km), at the same anchorage he had used the preceding summer. Here the ship is seen from inside an ice cavern on the foreshores of Commonwealth Bay.*

Mawson barely made it back to Cape Denison alive. He was so ravaged by his long journey, the last month of it alone, that when the few men that Captain Davis had left behind at Main Base ran up the hill to meet him they did not at first recognise which of the three missing men he was. This was not surprising considering Mawson had lost a third of his bodyweight.

When Mawson staggered into camp on 8 February, the adventure was not yet over. Captain Davis had arrived at Commonwealth Bay on 13 January to the enthusiastic greeting of those at Main Base. The sledging parties of Bage and then Bickerton arrived over the next few days and everyone was impatient for the arrival of Mawson, Ninnis and Mertz. Davis declared that he would have leave by 30 January to pick up Frank Wild's Western Party, two weeks after the pick-up date he had arranged with Mawson for Cape Denison. With Mawson's party a week overdue, Davis took the precaution of unloading coal and other supplies in case some expeditioners had to stay for a second winter. The collapsed wireless masts were re-erected – during the preceding year Main Base's unanswered transmissions had been received at Macquarie Island. Then *Aurora* searched the coast to the east for signs of life, with a radio receiver on board so Davis could be alerted to Mawson's return. This search proved fruitless, and Davis returned to Commonwealth Bay. The 30 January deadline came and went, and still Davis had *Aurora* weathering the gales off Cape Denison. On 8 February he decided he could wait no longer so he set *Aurora* on its 2400-kilometre journey to the west.

'Volunteers' had to be selected, as no-one wanted to stay but all would if so asked.

Eight hours after *Aurora* set off to relieve the Western party, Davis received a wireless message to 'return and collect all hands'. He swung the ship around and steamed to Commonwealth Bay, but conditions were dangerous and showed no signs of easing. Commonwealth Bay was living up to its newly established reputation as the windiest place in the world. Davis feared for Frank Wild's party, whose base was erected on a floating ice shelf, which the previous summer *Aurora* had reached only after difficult passage through the pack-ice. He knew that everyone at Cape Denison would be safe for the winter, so he made the heart-wrenching decision to head back to the west. Though he got everyone's agreement, some of the party felt that Davis should have tried to land a boat. Once he

again steamed away from Commonwealth Bay. For a week *Aurora* was driven west by an easterly gale. Visibility was poor, but luckily improved as they reached a zone of heavy pack-ice. The next obstacle was finding a course through the multitude of icebergs, which they were able to do without too many difficulties. On 23 February they reached the Shackleton Ice Shelf. Wild and his seven companions were waiting on the sea-ice, and after only a few hours their necessary belongings had been sledged down from the hut and loaded onto the ship. *Aurora* was set on a course for Macquarie Island, its only port of call before for Hobart. Increasing darkness and worsening ice conditions had by now made Cape Denison inaccessible until the next summer.

On board the men exchanged stories about the adventures of the preceding year. At the Grottoes, as the Western Party named their winter quarters, the men had also

When Davis reached the Shackleton Ice Shelf, the site of Frank Wild's Western Base, 2,400 kilometres west of Cape Denison, he took advantage of being anchored against an ice-floe to replenish the ship's water supplies. Ice was taken on board and melted.

When the Western Party boarded Aurora *they told stories of blizzards which rivalled those at Cape Denison. The hut that they assembled on the plateau at the top of the ice-cliffs was very quickly drifted over with snow until it was completely covered. Access was through a tunnel or a skylight designed with this in mind. Keeping the tunnel clear of snow was a constant battle.*

endured a bleak winter, but it had not been quite as consistently bad as that at Cape Denison. The hut was soon buried by snow, which was just as well, as during the winter they recorded winds of 160 kilometres per hour. Living as they did on a glacier with plenty of crevasses, much use was made of skis. Perhaps Wild also held a different view to Mawson about the benefits of skiing compared to its risks.

In August 1912, the Western Party laid the first depots for two successful, long journeys. Evan Jones led Archibald Hoadley and Dovers west on a sledge journey to Gaussberg, an extinct volcano first visited by Drygalksi's expedition ten years earlier. Frank Wild set off to the east with Alec Kennedy and Andrew Watson, with Charles Harrisson in support. The plan was that Harrisson would return to base alone at the end of the first week. However, when one of the Eastern Party's two sledges was blown away by a blizzard, Harrisson was obliged to make his sledge available, which meant he had to stay as well. Harrisson welcomed the adventure, but Morton Moyes, who was in charge of the hut, had been expecting him to return after two weeks. Moyes spent the next nine weeks alone, for seven of them he was convinced that Harrisson had perished in his attempt to return to The Grottoes. After travelling 190 kilometres from their base the Eastern Party were turned back by the Denman Glacier, which was so heavily crevassed that it was impassable.

Aurora arrived to collect them a year and one day after they had been dropped off. When the ship reached Macquarie Island, and the island party learnt of Mawson's predicament, all members on the island selflessly volunteered to stay for another year to maintain radio contact with Cape Denison.

The wireless message to Captain Davis announcing Mawson's lone return from the sledge journey had been sent from Commonwealth Bay by Sidney Jeffryes, the

The Grottoes looked like a snow cave from outside, but the buried hut was a cosy shelter with the latest conveniences available to expeditioners in 1911, except for a snowing machine, which had been mistakenly unloaded at Cape Denison.

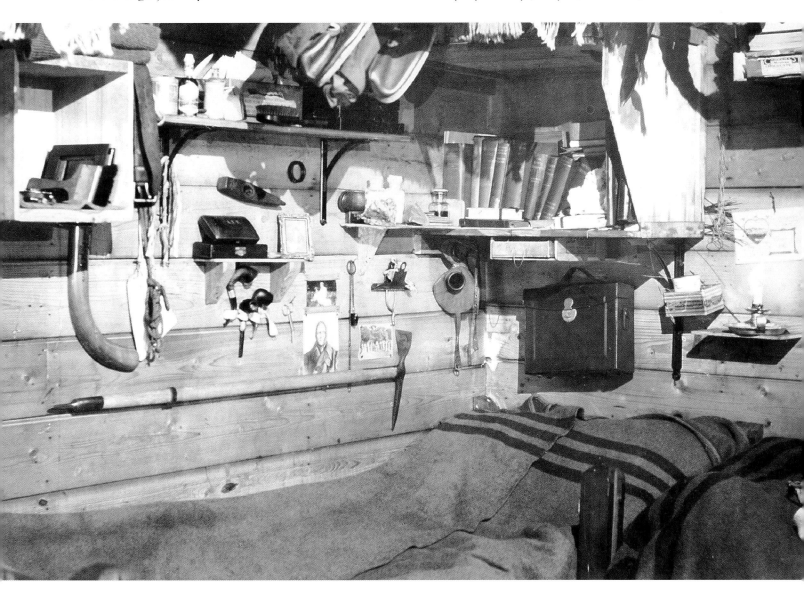

only new face at Main Base for the second year. On 22 February Mawson and his expeditioners learnt that Scott and four others had died when returning from the South Pole. On hearing this news Mawson wrote in his diary, 'I know what this means as I have been so near to it myself recently.'

Jeffryes was an enthusiastic and dedicated wireless operator, at least at first, but long-distance radio communications did not occur with any degree of consistency until March, when darkness began to return to Antarctica. Radio signals transmitted better at night, and Mawson noted that aurora australis interfered with wireless reception.

It took months for Mawson to recover from his ordeal. His insides were in turmoil from the poor diet, and the skin on much of his body had to regrow. His companions nursed him back to health, 'and vied with each other in making things as comfortable as possible for me'. Although Mawson was not capable of doing

To keep perpetually drifting snow out of the ice-shaft at The Grottoes the men built an igloo over the top of it. They hadn't mastered the technique of making a dome, so they used canvas as the roof.

much at first, he followed his hut-mates around, listening to their conversations, not talking, just appreciating their company.

During these months he no doubt wondered why Providence had spared him. The pioneering Antarctic sledge journeys of the Heroic Era were exceptionally demanding undertakings, physically because of the effort and the intense cold, and psychologically because of the sheer isolation and the pressures of being totally self-reliant in a poorly understood, unexplored continent. Mawson had coped well with these circumstances on the Magnetic Pole journey in 1908–09. At the end of that venture he still had energy to spare as well as clarity of mind, while Edgeworth David, almost twice Mawson's age, had neither. Mackay also had crumpled under the psychological pressure. In the last stages, Mackay had mutinied and forced David to hand over his leadership to Mawson, an act which only undermined their strength as a team.

On that expedition, Mawson had demonstrated his ability to perform in the extreme conditions of Antarctica for months on end. He had pushed himself beyond the normal limits of endurance and found that by refocusing his goals he could struggle onwards. Now, in the disastrous circumstances of his own expedition,

Frank Wild led a sledging journey to the east. They weathered blizzards and navigated around crevasses, but their progress was eventually stopped by the Denman Glacier, tortured mass crevasses and unstable ice blocks. Here they are moving the sledges across an old crevasse drifted full of snow at the edge of the glacier, shortly before realising the futility of their task.

Mawson benefited not only from his past sledging experience but also from the strength which came from leadership. Mertz had neither of these advantages. When Ninnis and their essential supplies had plunged into the crevasse, Mawson had been shouldering the full responsibility of the expedition for an entire year. He had faith in himself that he would make it all work. As leader, he was always ready to respond to the needs of the moment, and he approached his and Mertz's escape from the disaster with the same resolve. For the sake of Ninnis and Mertz, as well as Paquita, the expedition and, lastly, himself, Mawson was determined to make it back alive.

Mawson returned, and brought with him only his point of view. Until the last entry in Mertz's diary, Mertz had seemed strong, all things considered, and optimistic. Perhaps he had weakened more quickly without his protective burberry trousers. Perhaps, he had unwittingly eaten more dog livers with their toxic Vitamin A. Perhaps he was more deeply demoralised than he showed by the death of his close friend Ninnis. Others have theorised about these possibilities, and no doubt these questions about Mertz, and others we shall never know, plagued Mawson's mind during his second year at Cape Denison.

In late March, after six weeks of recuperating, Mawson wrote:

'I find my nerves are in a very serious state, and from the feeling I have in [the] base of my head I have a suspicion that I may go off my rocker very soon.' Fortunately he was wrong; it was someone else's sanity which did not stand the strain.

With the initial difficulties in transmitting wireless messages, Mawson felt duty-bound to contact his sponsors and others involved with the expedition as a matter of urgency, so it was not until April that he managed to send a message to Paquita. It read:

DEEPLY REGRET DELAY STOP ONLY JUST MANAGED TO REACH HUT STOP EFFECTS NOW GONE BUT LOST MOST MY HAIR STOP YOU ARE FREE TO CONSIDER YOUR CONTRACT BUT TRUST YOU WILL NOT ABANDON YOUR SECOND HAND DOUGLAS.

From the Western Base, a sledging party set off westwards for 200 kilometres to Gaussberg, an extinct volcano discovered by Drygalski's expedition, which gave them the opportunity to do some exploring when their ship was unintentionally trapped in the pack ice to the north for the winter. Here Jones stand on top of the 400 metre-high mountain, with his compass open and resting on the rock beside him.

With constant bad weather in the first three weeks of February 1913, the Western Base party were anxious about the arrival of Aurora, *wondering whether storms at sea and difficult pack-ice conditions would leave them stranded for another winter. Here they wave with delight as* Aurora *approaches on 23 February, a year and a day after they had been dropped off.*

The message was sent in morse code, relayed via Macquarie Island to a wireless service in Australia, then sent in decoded form to the recipient. The intimacy of this personal message, and others, was necessarily limited.

Paquita answered Mawson at once:

DEEPLY THANKFUL YOU ARE SAFE STOP WARMEST WELCOME AWAITING YOUR HAIRLESS RETURN STOP REGARDING CONTRACT SAME AS EVER ONLY MORE SO STOP THOUGHTS ALWAYS WITH YOU STOP ALL WELL HERE STOP MONTHS SOON PASS STOP TAKE THINGS EASIER THIS WINTER STOP SPEAK AS OFTEN AS POSSIBLE.

Mawson was much gratified to receive this reply, although 'months soon pass' was more the case in Adelaide than in Cape Denison. Much of the scientific work planned for the base had been completed, though there was always the weather to record. The wind blew even more strongly than it had done the preceding winter, with the climax being an eight-hour period when the wind averaged a speed of 170 kilometres per hour. During the winter each of the seven men found ways to keep occupied, if not exactly busy. There were always chores to be done, and there were now fewer men to share these among. Those tasks which required journeys outside were no less exciting than they had been the preceding winter. There were reports to write, journals to keep, maps to make. It was at this time that Mawson gave the names Ninnis Glacier and Mertz Glacier to the two great glaciers the three of them

At the end of the second winter at Cape Denison, the sea was frozen solid around the base of the ice-cliffs, allowing Mawson and his companions to explore these spectacular features.

In the Main Hut at Cape Denison, Bage repairs his sleeping bag while clothes air and dry above him.

The long shadow of the figure on the sea-ice west of the Land's End is typical of Antarctic spring when the days are still short and the sun is yet to rise high in the sky.

had crossed. McLean decided to produce ***The Adelie Blizzard***, a monthly publication for which, wrote Mawson, 'contributions were invited from all on every subject except the wind.' Someone submitted 'The Evolution of Women' which 'introduced us to a once-familiar subject.' As a doctor, McLean may have been concerned about the group's morale and saw the 'Blizzard' as a focus for everyone's attention.

McLean also busied himself on a project which he hoped would yield information about Antarctic tides. His method – a scientist must always have a method – was to put messages in bottles and dispatch them on the tide. As yet none have been recovered.

At first an invalid, Mawson was forced to take on the role of expedition leader again, although not under circumstances he enjoyed. Initially Jeffryes was very dedicated to his job as wireless operator, to the exclusion of almost everything else. Unfortunately, he proved to be mentally unstable. At first Mawson humoured him, as Jeffryes was the only person competent with Morse Code, but when he realised that Jeffryes, in a state of paranoia, had transmitted some very misleading messages, he replaced him with Bickerton, who was very slow with morse code.

ERECTED
TO COMMEMORATE
THE SUPREME SACRIFICE
MADE BY
LIEUT. B.E.S. NINNIS, R.F.
AND
DR. X. MERTZ
IN THE
CAUSE OF SCIENCE
—
A.A.E. 1913

There was more for everyone to do in spring. Mawson wrote:

'If the air was clear of drift (windblown snow), and the wind not over fifty miles per hour (80 km/h), one could spend a pleasant hour or more walking along the shore watching the birds and noting changes which were always occurring along our length of rocky shore.'

He also describes a very efficient fishing procedure, with which one afternoon two men landed 52 fish. They froze solid within minutes of being flipped out onto the sea-ice, and in this state were put in the larder until required by the cook.

Bickerton and Hodgeman had put much time into fashioning a memorial to Ninnis and Mertz. They bolted together a large cross out of solid oregon beams from the broken wireless mast, then bound it with brass. During a break in the weather the cross was erected at Azimuth Hill, on top of the rocky ridge to the west of the hut. A wooden plaque was placed among the many rocks heaped around its base. Everyone was confident it would resist the worst weather that Cape Denison could throw at it for a hundred years or more.

One of *Aurora*'s surprise deliveries was a team of Greenland dogs which had been to the South Pole. Roald Amundsen had given them to Davis when his ship *Fram* had pulled into Hobart. With the help of the dogs, Mawson, Madigan and Hodgeman set out on a sledge journey in November. Their first goal was Mt Murchison, where they found that a three-metre pole which had been placed on the summit the previous summer was almost totally buried by snow. They pushed on in search of a depot left by Madigan's and Bage's parties, but they were frustrated yet again by bad weather – but this was the last blizzard they would have at Commonwealth Bay. When they were descending from Aladdin's Cave they spotted *Aurora* in the distance.

It was an emotional reunion for Davis and Mawson in particular, and all the shore party were delighted to see Frank Hurley, Johnnie Hunter and Percy Correll again. That night they sat down to dinner at a white tablecloth and were served fresh mutton and vegetables. The trappings of civilisation had reached them at last. Also on board were George Ainsworth and his team-mates from the Macquarie Island base, also ready for home after two years away. *Aurora* headed north from Commonwealth Bay as soon as equipment and specimens from the hut were loaded and stowed, but home was not their first destination. Further marine survey work was scheduled to be completed first, and a harrowing time was had with pack-ice

During the winter Bickerton made a memorial cross out of solid oregon beams from the broken wireless mast and then bound it with brass, while Hodgeman chiselled and carved a plaque, using wood from the dining table, which they'd cut in half now that it no longer needed to sit 18 men.

During December 1913 there was some unplanned excitement when the roof above the stove caught alight. Here the fire brigade is in action, with Mawson in dark trousers turning towards the camera.

A typical sledging scene on the plateau above Cape Denison. In late November, Mawson led a party inland to try to recover some instruments cached the previous summer, but they were turned back by blizzards. While descending from the plateau close to midnight on 12 December, their extra height above sea level allowed them to spot the distant Aurora *some hours ahead of their companions at Main Base.*

As Aurora *approached Antarctica, Harold Hamilton, biologist with the Macquarie Island team, took advantage of the fact that pack-ice dampens the swell of the sea. Here he samples the life of Antarctic waters with a hand-net.*

and icebergs as they explored the seas to the west of Frank Wild's base. Finally a course was set for Adelaide, which they approached on 26 February 1914.

As the ship stood offshore waiting daytime entry to the harbour, it must have been with a sense of trepidation that Mawson pondered his reception. On his return from Shackleton's expedition in 1909 he had been hailed as a hero. Circumstances were very different this time. Two people had died. He had returned a year late, at extra costs which he couldn't even begin to consider. He had landed only two bases on the continent rather than the three he had planned, and his explorations and scientific work had been curtailed by the bad weather. His hopes of charting thousands of kilometres of unknown coast had been foiled by heavy pack-ice. Would the public's excitement at the expedition's return have been expended the previous summer when the main body of expeditioners came home? Would he be seen as a failure? How would Paquita respond to him, and he to her?

After two years on the ice, one of them unplanned, Douglas Mawson, wearing knee-high boots, has aged more than the two years which had elapsed. Kneeling in front of Mawson on the deck of Aurora *is Frank Hurley.*

CHAPTER 8

Mawson
of the
Antarctic

*While in London, Mawson, aged 32, was knighted
by King George V, who showed considerable
interest in Mawson's Antarctic discoveries.
The region encompassing Cape Denison was
named King George V Land. This photograph
of Sir Douglas on the occasion of his knighting
shows him in full regalia.*

Mawson's reservations about how he would be received were, of course, ill-founded. Again he was greeted as a hero, with two public receptions, one a glorious event at Adelaide Town Hall and the other at the university, with the latter attended by the Governor-General, Lord Denman. The press was worshipful, and Paquita was pleased to see her fiancé again. The Delprat family had moved to Melbourne during 1913, but Paquita and her mother returned to Adelaide to meet Mawson, who had told Paquita more than two years earlier to expect the ship around 26 or 27 February. She assumed, correctly, that this estimate would apply to the second year as well as the first. As soon as they disembarked, Mawson, accompanied by Captain Davis, went to the Australia Hotel were the Delprats had taken a suite of rooms. Davis and Mrs Delprat sat on the balcony and

On 31 March 1914, Douglas Mawson and Francesca (Paquita) Delprat were married in Holy Trinity Church of England in Melbourne. From the left, the women are Hester Berry (bridesmaid), Paquita Mawson, H. Delprat (bride's mother) Elizabeth (Carmen) Delprat (bride's sister), and the men are J. K. Davis (best man), William Mawson (boasting the Mawson hairline), Douglas Mawson, G. D. Delprat (bride's father),

"RACING WITH DEATH
IN
ANTARCTIC BLIZZARDS"

ILLUSTRATED LECTURE
By SIR DOUGLAS MAWSON, K. B., D. Sc., B. E.

DR. X. MERTZ
One of Sir Douglas Mawson's comrades on the sledge journey, who lost his life from exposure and exhaustion.

SIR DOUGLAS MAWSON
Leader of the Expedition and the sole survivor of the tragic sledging journey.

**LIEUT. B. E. S. NINNIS,
ROYAL FUSILIERS**
Sir Douglas Mawson's other comrade, lost by falling into a crevasse with his sledge and dogs.

In this Lecture Sir Douglas Mawson tells the story of his thrilling experiences in the Antarctic regions, in the course of which both his companions lost their lives, and he himself, after perhaps the most terrific perils out of which any adventurer ever escaped alive, was just able to reach safety. The lecture is fully illustrated with the most remarkable Still and Motion Pictures ever taken in Polar Regions.

The unplanned second winter in Antarctic put the Australasian Antarctic Expedition into serious debt. Mawson helped pay off these debts by giving illustrated lectures in Australia, Britain and America. He gave only two lectures in Europe before the outbreak of The Great War ruled out the possibility of any others.

Although he may have dressed like a serious scientist, and he certainly had the qualifications of one, he didn't always behave like one, even when on the grounds of the Delprat Mansion in Melbourne. Here Mawson holds his first child, Patricia, using the method favoured by cats with their kittens.

discussed Antarctica and Australia, while Douglas and Paquita walked outside to talk. They quickly established that the feelings they had nursed for each other for 28 months of separation withstood the reality of being together again, and a wedding date was set within the month. The tenor of their life together, at least for the next six months, was set when they went to the cable office together so that Mawson could dictate a press release – about the expedition rather than his marriage – for the Australian and London papers.

Mawson's other preoccupation at this time was not as joyous. Although he had spoken of the possibility of being trapped in Antarctica for a second winter and had taken some precautions in the form of extra provisions, he had not made any plans to fund *Aurora*'s third consecutive southern summer voyage. The Commonwealth Government had helped fund this with a grant of £5000, but even so Mawson returned home to a debt of £8000. This was almost halved by the quick sale of **Aurora** to Shackleton for his upcoming Imperial Transantarctic Expedition. But now Mawson needed to raise the balance, as well as extra money to produce the expedition reports which, from his point of view, were the justification for the expedition. Mawson saw that his best chance lay in getting his account of the expedition published in Britain, where contact had already been made with William

Heinemann and where there were other important loose ends to be tied up. He made plans for a working honeymoon, booking passage for himself and Paquita on *Orama*, bound for Marseilles.

First came their marriage, at Holy Trinity Church of England in Melbourne. Paquita wore a necklace of black opals, which was a beautiful gift from a husband whose other love was geology. J. K. Davis was best man, with other members of the expedition in attendance. University Registrar Charles Hodge came across from Adelaide, and T.W. Edgeworth David rushed down from Sydney, as did Mawson's brother, William. With the recent death of their father and their mother unable to travel due to illness, William was the only representative of the family. The reception was held in the gardens of the Delprat's Toorak home and, as might be expected, had an Antarctic theme. Both bride and groom were tall and striking, and with their interesting backgrounds, became the couple of the moment. However, neither Melbourne nor Adelaide society had the chance to capitalise on

Not long after the birth of his first child, Mawson returned to England to help the war effort. Working in the British Ministry of Munitions, he attained the rank of Major. Paquita Mawson later followed her husband to Britain, leaving Patricia in the care of her family.

The Mawsons returned to Australia on board SS Euripedes, *as did Edgeworth David, seen here on deck with Mawson. David had served with the Australian tunnelling force until he was injured by falling 20 metres down a shaft. He was then evacuated to England to recuperate.*

the wedding because the next day, 1 April 1914, Dr. and Mrs Mawson boarded *Orama* bound for England.

Barely a month after returning from Antarctica, Mawson was again on the high seas. It wasn't exactly a normal honeymoon, but at least there were no icebergs. Also on board were Captain Davis and Archie McLean. Mawson had engaged McLean, who had edited with much enthusiasm *The Adelie Blizzard*, during their second winter in Antarctica, to edit the first draft of *Home of the Blizzard,* the popular account of the expedition. Mawson was the chief author of the book, but there were contributions from other expedition members. He hoped that royalties from book sales would substantially reduce the expedition debt.

The newlyweds did enjoy the cruise, although Mawson remained very interested in scientific matters. When the captain's cat wandered into their cabin, for example,

Mawson tested the bleaching properties of hydrogen peroxide on its tail, but the cat escaped before he could view the effect. Mawson was also preoccupied with the expedition book, and with preparing the illustrated lecture which he would give many times in Britain and the United States. In Marseilles they were met by William Heinemann, the publisher of the proposed book, who discussed the project with Mawson all the way to Paris. After a function and ceremony in Paris they crossed from Calais to Dover and went on to London. At Victoria Station they were intercepted by Antarctic colleagues and the Press. The swirl of social, scientific and Antarctic networking had begun. More important was the private matter of meeting with the family of Belgrave Ninnis, which they did at the first opportunity.

At an interview with King George V before being knighted, Mawson was asked

A gift from BHP at Port Pirie, two slag pots here hold pot plants on the front steps of the Jerbii, Mawson's Brighton home which he designed during an Antarctic winter and built on land given to the Mawsons by Paquita's father, G.D. Delprat. This photo was taken many years after the house was built, as the boy on the steps is Andrew McEwin, one of the Mawson's grandsons.

many questions by the King about the newly discovered Antarctic lands, one of which now bore his name. Mawson was also received by Queen Alexandra and the Empress of Russia. A luncheon held for him by Sir George Reid, Australian High Commissioner at the British Empire Club, was attended by many nobles and notables, including Lord Tennyson.

While Mawson had been in Antarctica, Paquita had travelled to Europe with her mother, who was from a well-to-do Dutch family, so she was accustomed to travel, but not at all familiar with the high society that she became party to because of her husband's achievements. At one function, while Douglas was elsewhere engaged, she gave her name as Mrs Mawson and was announced as such. Her hostess quickly reprimanded her: 'Your husband was knighted this morning, my dear. You must be announced properly!'

It is difficult to know what Mawson made of all this fuss, and although it seems he knew and liked the etiquette, he was most likely wondering how the attention could best be used to help reduce the expedition debt. As a fundraising exercise the journey to Britain was not as profitable as he had hoped, although his close friend Kathleen Scott privately gave Mawson £1000 from the proceeds of Scott's ***Last***

When Mawson bought some timbered acreage east of Adelaide to develop his interests in forestry and farming, he named the property Harewood after the estate which had been farmed by the Mawsons of Yorkshire, Seen here in its early days with Patricia (left) and Jessica, Harewood eventually boasted magnificent trees from many parts of the world.

Expedition, her husband's diaries, which had been published in 1913. Lady Scott felt it appropriate that the money earned from the diaries be returned to the cause of Antarctic exploration.

In London, Mawson gave a presentation to the Royal Geographical Society, which many expedition members attended, and which was very well received by the luminaries of the day. The expedition was lauded as the greatest scientific expedition yet conducted in Antarctica, an accolade which was particularly important to him.

For Mawson these presentations were demanding events, where form and procedure were as important as content. Luckily, Davis was often present, and while Mawson was preoccupied, Davis was able to advise Lady Mawson on matters of protocol. To his embarrassment and amusement, Paquita told Davis that she could never have survived the honeymoon without him. By some accounts she was a woman who spoke her mind, which no doubt was one reason she was attractive to Douglas, who also had his own way of doing things.

The Mawsons began their return journey to Australia by travelling to the Netherlands to meet Paquita's relatives. Then they continued to Switzerland to meet the family of Xavier Mertz, prominent industrialists in Basel, who remained inconsolable eighteen months after hearing the news of their son's death. At Toulon they caught a ship back to Australia, arriving in late July 1914.

Although Mawson was certainly welcomed and acknowledged in Britain, the Antarctic hero of the day was Scott, who had died for England in a blizzard. The last message of Scott's diary reads: 'I do not regret this journey, which has shown that Englishmen can endure hardships, help one another, and meet death with as great a fortitude as ever in the past.' It was hard act to follow. If Mawson had accepted Scott's invitation to join him on his push for the Pole, perhaps his strength and focus might have brought them through alive.

In any case, Mawson was more interested in the Australasian Antarctic Expedition's achievements being recognised by the world's scientific community. This recognition came in 1915, when the Royal Geographical Society awarded him the Founder's Gold Medal. Much as he valued this highest of all RGS honours, he knew that, as with all scientific matters, the true worth lay in publishing the expedition's findings so other scientists could build on the knowledge. This task was to take up much of Mawson's time and energy for many years to come.

For several years Mawson had either been away from Adelaide or distracted by his expedition. He now applied himself to his university work, but at the end of the teaching term he and Paquita headed north again for Mawson's planned lecture tours in Europe and the US. With the outbreak of the Great War, Europe was obviously out of the question; even the journey around Cape Horn and northwards into the Atlantic Ocean was affected, as there was the continual threat of German warships. First stop was London, from where Paquita returned to Australia almost immediately, pregnant with their first child. Mawson had hoped to be back from the US in time for the birth but was delayed by lucrative engagements. He wrote home almost daily. At last, in mid-1915, he returned to Melbourne to meet his newborn daughter, Patricia, and went with his new family to Adelaide. He again took up his work at the university, and put as much time as he could into preparing the expedition's scientific results for publication. He also took up the cause of conscription,

The Mawson girls and some cousins partici-pate, if not exactly help, with the clearing of land on Harewood. The Mawson's were not entirely happy with the schooling options available for their daughters in Adelaide. Paquita home schooled the girls using teaching materials mailed from England, as suitable resources were not then available in Australia. When Patricia and Jessica later attended Woodlands Church of England Grammar School, Mawson petitioned the head-mistress to give his girls more schooling in arithmetic and sci-ence (not a subject then considered an appropriate career for girls) and less in religious studies and sewing – a classic example of Mawson paying attention to details and modifying those which did not suit his vision.

as he clearly felt strongly about each man doing his duty, and was encouraged in this by Edgeworth David. He soon decided that he must serve in the war himself, but found that the Australian defence forces could offer nothing to a man who had proved himself as a leader in the most difficult of circumstances and was also scientist and a knight.

So Mawson went to London, arriving in early May 1916. Here, too, there were many men with reputations looking for suitable military positions. As soon as he stepped off the ship Mawson was informed by the British Admiralty that he had been placed on a committee to plan the rescue of Ernest Shackleton's Imperial Transantarctic Expedition (of which Frank Wild and Frank Hurley were members). Shackleton had planned to land two parties on the continent, one using *Aurora* at the Ross Sea (which would lay depots inland), and one which would undertake the crossing from the Weddel Sea after being dropped off by *Endurance*. For two years there had been no word of the expedition. Mawson's appointment to the committee, without being consulted, was recognition of his unequalled qualifications as an Antarctic explorer. (The only person with equal abilities was Davis, who also played a role, rescuing the survivors of the Ross Sea party.) The committee's brief was to organise two rescue missions, and much work was done with budgets and logistics. Mawson even considered leading the expedition.

The Mawson girls and some cousins participate, if not exactly help, with the clearing of land on Harewood.

Then, on 31 May, word came from Shackleton on the Falkland Islands. His news was that all who had been on board *Endurance* were safe but the crew at Ross Island needed to be picked up from Antarctica. An epic story of survival unfolded. *Endurance* had been trapped in the pack-ice of the Weddel Sea for 10 months before being crushed and sunk. Shackleton and his team were stranded on the drifting ice for almost five months with supplies

and the ship's boats. A desperate yet successful bid was made to reach Elephant Island, where they landed on a rocky beach beneath unscaleable cliffs. Leaving most of his crew under the charge of Frank Wild, Shackleton and five men set out in an open boat on a 1300-kilometre journey to South Georgia, the southernmost outpost of the British Empire. One hundred and five days after leaving his men, Shackleton returned to Elephant Island with a rescue vessel. The committee for the Shackleton Relief Expedition now faced the much simpler task of sending Captain Davis south to recover the team left at Ross Island.

Mawson returned to the war effort, or at least to his effort to join it. He finally obtained a position that required some of his skills. Based in Liverpool, he liaised between the Ministry of Munitions and the Russian Government Committee, working in the Explosives Division and attaining the rank of Major. Later in 1916, Paquita travelled to England via the United States, where she left young Patricia in the care of her mother, who was staying with another of her daughters in San Francisco. Paquita's arrival lifted Douglas' spirits enormously. She soon found

In many parts of South Australia, Mawson was a well-known figure because of his frequent field trips. Here he is seen with Mr Coulston, overseer of Plumbago Station, one of many places Mawson often visited in the course of his field work.

volunteer work with a group of women making hospital dressings out of sphagnum moss, and also helped Douglas with his secretarial work. Paquita renewed contact with Mrs Ninnis who confided to Paquita that she had come to terms with her son's death in Antarctica. His regiment had been slaughtered in France; sudden death in an icy crevasse, during a great adventure, was better than the carnage in the mud at Flanders.

When Mawson became Head of the Explosives Department in London, he and Paquita decided to live in a small cottage in the country by the Thames. Mawson was also the Russian Government's Munitions Intelligence Officer. He had varied responsibilities, but found most aspects of his work tedious, and was torn between returning to Adelaide to publish A.A.E. reports and staying in London to help in his small way with the war. He chose to stay, experiencing the joy of the birth of their second daughter, Jessica, in October 1917 and witnessing the armistice on 11 November 1918.

They sailed back to Australia during March and April, disembarking in Melbourne. Paquita stayed with the girls at her parents' house, where Patricia had lived since returning with her grandmother from San Francisco. Mawson went back to Adelaide, where he immediately jumped back into university life and set about organising a home for his family. He rented a house at the beach suburb of Brighton, where they would live until they built their own home on land later to be given to them by Paquita's father. Over the next year they built a more modest version of the house Mawson had designed during long nights as nightwatchman in the hut at Cape Denison.

The next ten years were a time of consolidation for Mawson. The preceding decade had been filled with the A.A.E. and its aftermath, and then with the war. The expedition debts had been much harder to clear because of the war. Book sales, the expedition film and his lectures all returned far less money than would have been the case in happier times. Europe would have been a good market for all of these, but rather than books and lectures, Mawson had helped to supply Allied forces in Europe with weapons through the British Ministry of Munitions.

Back in Adelaide, Mawson was eager to pursue his geology, not only to consolidate his career but because he loved it. He particularly enjoyed field work, and spent a great deal of time in the Flinders Ranges, much of it with his students. One of his main areas of study was the Precambrian regions of the Flinders Ranges,

which were more than 600 million years old, particularly those places which had been subjected to glaciation. It had been these areas which, back in 1907, had first sparked his interest in visiting Antarctica with Shackleton.

The nature of Mawson's work at the University of Adelaide changed when Honorary Professor Walter Howchin retired in 1921. Mawson was appointed to the newly created chair of Geology and Mineralogy. He saw his role as creating a geology department which offered a complete geology course, rather than the less co-ordinated courses he and Howchin had offered previously. Both were gifted and very knowledgeable geologists, but it was now up to Mawson to introduce a fully integrated course. Mawson found himself lecturing in all subjects, and when it came to unfamiliar topics, he had much time-consuming preparation to do. He rescued himself from this very heavy workload by recruiting Dr. Cecil Madigan, who had led the Eastern Coastal Sledging Party in 1912 and had stayed with Mawson for the second winter at Cape Denison. Mawson was so impressed with Madigan that he lured him back from the Sudan, where he was working as a

On a camping trip to the Coorong, one of South Australia's first national parks, Sir Douglas gleefully 'assists' Lady Mawson into their boat by slapping her backside. His hand raised ready to slap disappears out of the top of the photo.

geologist, with the offer of a lectureship and the chance to help shape Mawson's vision for the geology department. The two of them worked together for the next 18 years. According to Arthur Alderman, who was a student under both men and went on to work with them in the department, and who eventually took over Mawson's professorship in 1953, they were very much alike.

'Each was fundamentally an explorer in whom the excitement of penetrating unknown regions was completely alloyed with the urge for scientific discovery. They both had a high sense of duty and similar ideas on politics and ethical and academic standards.'

Madigan, however, was always to stand in the shadow of Mawson, who was already internationally known and respected.

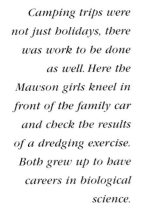

Camping trips were not just holidays, there was work to be done as well. Here the Mawson girls kneel in front of the family car and check the results of a dredging exercise. Both grew up to have careers in biological science.

In 1920 Mawson had been honoured with an OBE, and in 1923, was elected Fellow of the Royal Society, in recognition of the work he had done in the New Hebrides, the Barrier Ranges and, of course, Antarctica. He was a prominent member of the Australian Association for the Advancement of Science, with which he had been involved since 1906, and was a member of many other committees and scientific bodies, including the Australian National Research Council. Another of his interests, something for which he lobbied hard, with eventual success in 1933, was that Macquarie Island be made a conservation area to prevent penguins and seals being exterminated by uncontrolled slaughter for their oil.

Mawson's life was busy not only with these matters. He was a man who paid attention to detail, and while building their family home at Brighton he had made items of furniture and became interested in the uses of different kinds of timber. This interest encouraged him to purchase several blocks of land in the Kuitpo Forest, 50 kilometres south-east of Brighton, where he harvested timber and then replanted. With the proceeds he and two partners built a sawmill and sold the produce through their company, South Australian Hardwoods. This was just a sideline; one he was very interested in, but a sideline nevertheless. Meanwhile, once he had bought the land at the edge of the Kuitpo forest, he investigated not only the horticultural and

At West India Docks in London, Sir Douglas helps the Duchess of York (who would become Queen Mother) with a wolf-skin mitt when she inspects Scott's old ship, Discovery, *which Mawson is outfitting for the BANZARE voyages. The Duke of York is also present. Having heard about the traditional expedition food, pemmican, the Duchess asked if she could taste some, although discouraged by the Duke. She found it quite palatable.*

financial aspects of forestry, but also the farming of sheep, pigs and cattle. He named the property 'Harewood', after the Harewood estates in Yorkshire where the Mawsons had farmed. The influence of his father can be seen in this development – his father had experimented with farming when Mawson was a boy, then taken a job in the office of a timberyard, followed by his more exotic farming ventures in New Guinea. Robert Mawson had died in November 1912, when Mawson was in Antarctica. Uncannily, a dream about his father had come to him at this time, during his long sledge journey and not long before the disaster which claimed Ninnis' life. (Mawson's mother died during World War I).

Interestingly, Mawson now exhibited the same entrepreneurial streak that had been prominent in his father. He achieved moderate success, but he really was too busy to become a successful businessman, or perhaps like his father, he was not destined to be wealthy, despite his best efforts. Much of the time that wasn't absorbed by work was devoted to his family. He paid close attention to his daughters' schooling and made sure that they were informed and involved with the development of Harewood. The example of a thorough scientific mind, he thought, produces more scientific minds. He was proven right. At a time when it much less common for women to have careers, both daughters graduated with science degrees. Jessica then worked as a microbiologist at Adelaide Hospital, while Patricia attained her Master of Science and worked as a zoologist.

Mawson's working life was full at many levels. Both his teaching work and his own geological studies involved field trips. He had a strong interest in minerals, cultivated by his first job at the university as a lecturer in mineralogy and petrology. This interest fostered his research in the mineral-rich arc of Precambrian rocks, more than 600 million years old, which stretch from Broken Hill through the Barrier Ranges into eastern South Australia. After many surveys across this wide area he was able to classify the rocks into two broad groups, the older group being highly metamorphosed by intense heat and the younger group less metamorphosed (its sedimentary origins were still obvious). Interestingly, given that indigenous Australians were shown little respect during these times, he called the younger group of rocks the Torrawangee Series and the older group the Willyama Complex, the latter being the Aboriginal name for Broken Hill. Mawson's field observations and his deductions from them, including those of the age of the rocks, have stood the test of modern radiometric techniques.

Paquita Mawson was an elegant, independent-minded woman, well-accustomed to making her own decisions. She travelled widely with her husband, but she also travelled in Europe without him (with a sister or a friend) when Mawson was occupied with his work. 'My letters were an interest to Douglas though he disapproved of my intention of skiing,' she wrote about her travels in Europe in 1937. "He thought me too old for this. I did learn, however, and enjoyed it immensely."

While involved with this research Mawson was also busy with the publishing of the Australasian Antarctic Expedition reports. This enormous job of the reports was always in his mind, sometimes prominently. The main reason for it being such a protracted exercise was lack of money. The last of 18 reports published was in 1947, and some subjects were never written up and published. In desperation, Mawson finally struck a deal in 1920 with the Government of New South Wales that involved the reports being produced by the Government Printer, in return for Antarctic specimens being lodged in the Australian Museum and records at the Mitchell Library. However, the terms of this were frequently renegotiated in following years, and Mawson was constantly badgering the relevant scientists to deliver their mansucripts and illustrations to the printers.

In 1928 Mawson was invited to investigate the feasibility of a huge hydroelectric scheme to dam Lake Manapouri in New Zealand's South Island; the scheme would generate sufficient power to support several new energy-hungry industries to be set up in the region. Mawson went to New Zealand to examine the site and became very enthusiastic about the project. Mawson was an all-or-nothing sort of man, and on this occasion he gave it his all, to the extent of travelling to London to attempt to raise finance to the order of £7 million. He raised considerable interest, but this was deflated by a change in the New Zealand government – the new party did not support the scheme. The nails were put in the coffin by the arrival of the Great Depression. Mawson held hopes for an eventual resurrection, but meanwhile his mind was taken off this unsatisfactory state of affairs by the prospect of another Antarctic expedition, one which was even grander in scope – but less life-threatening, he hoped – than the A.A.E. had been.

CHAPTER 9

For King *and* Country – *BANZARE*

Frank Hurley specialised in hanging off the most precarious parts of the ship to take photographs of it – this photo of Discovery *was taken from the bowsprit. Once during wild seas, Hurley was ordered down from the rigging by Captain MacKenzie who didn't want to bear the responsibility of Hurley seriously injuring himself or falling overboard. Hurley wrote a note freeing MacKenzie of all blame should he hurt himself, signed it, handed it to the captain, then climbed back up to the top of the mast.*

The vessel chosen for the BANZARE was Discovery, *seen at Cardiff before the voyage south to Cape Town. The vessel was chosen because it was available at no cost from the British government, even though it had the reputation of rolling excessively in rough seas and being inefficiently rigged for sailing. The ship had been purpose-built for Scott's first Antarctic voyage in 1901-04.*

Mawson witnessed sealing parties slay whole seal colonies, including mothers and their calves. Although he supported harvesting the living resources of the Antarctic in a sustainable fashion, Mawson was dismayed by such widespread slaughter and pushed strongly for conservation reserves and the regulation of all such industries. The BANZARE voyages were a means to obtaining the authority to regulate such exploitation.

With increased whaling activity in the southern oceans it was almost inevitable that an Australian expedition that had both political and economic goals would take place. The expedition was the British, Australian and New Zealand Antarctic Research Expedition, commonly referred to as BANZARE. Mawson was a key figure in the expedition's evolution, so it is not surprising that it also had a strong scientific program.

BANZARE had mixed origins. Whaling was an Antarctic industry that was already lucrative by the 1920s, and Britain and the Commonwealth nations did not want to miss out on the commercial potential not only of whaling but of other resources in the region. In 1923 the British Government had created what it called the Ross Sea Dependency, which operated on the same charter as the Falkland Island Dependencies, which had been declared in 1908. Both dependencies regulated whaling by licensing whalers, prohibiting the killing of females and calves, and limiting the number of killings. Implementation of the regulations was difficult – less so for British whalers who were under the jurisdiction of the British government – and Scott's old ship *Discovery* was based in the Falklands for this purpose. The declaration of these dependencies elevated competition in whaling from disputes between ships of different nations to discussions between diplomats and politicians.

For many years Mawson had been lobbying for regulation of the harvesting of seals and penguins, because after witnessing the slaughter on Macquarie Island, he feared that these species would become extinct. As a practical man, he believed in harvesting sea animals, including whales, but in a planned and sustainable fashion. In these views he was ahead of his time, and it must be remembered that the highly evolved intelligence of whales was several decades from being scientifically

A load of coal briquettes being swung aboard Discovery *at Cardiff. The greatest short-coming of* Discovery *was its limited coal-carrying capacity. Sails were essentially an auxiliary form of propulsion, particularly limited amongst pack-ice where manoeuvrability was important.*

established. Mawson also had strong views on Antarctic political issues. When the French laid claim to Adelie Land in 1924, Mawson vigorously opposed the claim. Although Durmont d'Urville had landed on an offshore island in 1840 and had claimed the region for France, Mawson argued that the presence of the A.A.E. on the continent for two years in this vicinity carried much more weight in terms of sovereignty. John King Davis also objected to the French claim. Davis had adopted Australia as his home, and in 1920 had been appointed to the post of Commonwealth Director of Navigation. (Coincidentally, in the early 1920s, he had proposed an Antarctic research expedition to the coast further west than that explored by the A.A.E. but the idea had not been taken up.)

What galvanised the Australian government into action was the Imperial Conference of Commonwealth Countries in 1926, held in London, where one of the

When Discovery *left Cardiff, Davis asked the crew to search for stowaways, a common phenomenon in depressed Britain in the late 1920s, and one which points to the limited options for escape. This boy hiding in a lifebuoy, who gave his name as Sutton, had boarded the ship at London. The ship returned to Cardiff to put him ashore.*

Discovery *docked at Cape Town, with the summit of Table Mountain hidden in clouds behind, and waited for the bulk of the expedition team to arrive from Australia via passenger liner across the Indian Ocean.*

Scientific work began almost as soon as Discovery *put to sea, with trawling for surface life, and the banding of birds that were captured, such as this young albatross.*

major issues was the question of territorial rights in Antarctic waters and on the continent itself. This led to the Australian National Research Council setting up an Antarctic Committee. Mawson had been a member of the Council since 1919, and of course he was appointed to the committee. A decision was soon reached that Mawson would lead a research expedition, with Davis in charge of the ship, with the charter of exploring the Antarctic lands and seas to the south of Australia and claiming them for the British Crown. However, when plans for the expedition were made public, no mention was made of the territorial agenda, but such is the way of politics. Science and exploration were the public smokescreen.

After some negotiation, it was decided that ***Discovery*** was the best vessel for the proposed expedition, which was to be conducted over the summers of 1929–30 and 1930–31. At the time the ship was performing its whaling work out of the Falklands, but it was sailed north to England for a special refit to meet BANZARE's needs. Mawson and Davis went to England to oversee this, and also to raise sponsorship funds, the ship having been lent by the British government. The Australian government was also providing funding, but it was still necessary to raise extra money and minimise costs by asking for sponsorship in kind. Having spent many years attending to debts and obligations of many sorts after the A.A.E., Mawson was determined to avoid all such burdens with this expedition and costs would be kept lower by working only from the ship. This was one reason why **Discovery** had been chosen for the job – it had already been refitted as a research vessel, although specifically for whaling and sealing. The disadvantage of the refit was that it severely reduced the ship's carrying capacity, especially when it came to coal. Captain Davis and Mawson discussed various schemes to overcome this problem, and the two which were implemented worked with limited degrees of success.

Mawson was very enthusiastic about the research work which could be done in regions which had rarely, if ever, been visited, but he was also motivated by his wish to plant the British flag on the untrodden stretches of the Antarctic coast, which lay only 2500 kilometres south of Australia. He decided that the first of the two voyages would depart from Cape Town, and on the way south coal would be loaded at Isle de Kerguelen, an old French whaling base in the southern Indian Ocean. Mawson left Davis and Frank Hurley in England and returned to Australia to tend to the many other matters which could only be arranged in Australia. For Mawson it was a pleasant change to be able to share the burden of organising the expedition with

Sailor A. B. McClennan with the fo'c'stle pets Nigger and Tiger, who were to raise a family on the voyage. One of the cats fell overboard in the cold southern latitudes and McClennan jumped into the water to save it.

the Antarctic Committee. As well as meeting his university commitments, Mawson worked extraordinarily hard on all sorts of expedition matters. He was the kind of man who liked to have a hand in everything simply because he was interested in everything. The expedition kept him so busy that when he finally boarded the ocean liner *Nestor* in Adelaide, bound for South Africa, he had piles of last-minute paperwork which he would have to post from Fremantle or Durban, as well as a geological paper about Central Australia which he had to finish writing during the passage to Cape Town.

After crossing the Indian Ocean, the ship was delayed in Durban, so it wasn't until 13 October 1929 that the entire expedition was united in Cape Town. Mawson and Davis had heated differences in opinion about several matters, which is not surprising with the expedition being organised by both of them on opposite sides of the globe. Mawson was pleased to see Frank Hurley, now an internationally acclaimed photographer. Not only was Hurley's constant enthusiasm good for morale, but Mawson could also be assured of good photographs and cinematic footage of the expedition.

The biologists on board were kept busy sorting the catch from trawling. Plankton, fish and seaweeds were sorted and identified, with a representative specimen of each preserved for reference where possible.

A group of scientists and sheathbill birds during lunchtime on the Crozet Islands. Left to right, standing: Marr, Harvey Johnston, Ingram. Front: Moyes, Douglas, Campbell, Mawson, Falla, Fletcher.

Heard Island's few beaches offer only exposed and dangerous landings, except in rare calm conditions. For this reason, Mawson decided to put a party, including himself, ashore for nine days. This was not a popular move with Captain Davis, who was keen to get to Antarctica proper to conduct what he saw as the expedition's main focus – exploration and mapping.

A Norwegian expedition on a similar mission to BANZARE had recently left Cape Town on *Norvegia*, which was owned by whaler Lars Christensen. The Norwegians were open about their territorial goals, but Mawson was not permitted to speak of BANZARE's non-research goals, which encouraged much speculation in the press.

'Apparently they are out to race,' he was widely quoted as saying, 'and are working in secret as Amundsen did when he beat Scott to the South Pole. However, I prefer not to discuss the matter. We are going to carry out a very carefully planned scientific programme.'

Not surprisingly, these comments inflamed sentiments in both Britain and Norway but Mawson was not in a position to defuse the situation. Mawson wired England with the request that BANZARE's full mission, including the territorial agenda as outlined to him by Australian Prime Minister Bruce, be made public. On 19 October, before receiving a reply, *Discovery* sailed out of Cape Town, leaving the diplomatic incident to the diplomats.

Discovery was infamous for the way it rolled at sea, a characteristic which everyone on board just had to accept. Nor was it a fast ship. A planned stop at Marion Island was forgone to make up for lost time, so the first stops were the French territories of Îles Crozet and Îles Kerguelen, where the biologists were kept busy cataloguing seals, birds and marine life. Arrangements had been made for the shipping of 400 tonnes of coal briquettes to Kerguelen, and these were duly located and loaded.

Next stop was Heard Island, a British possession dominated by the active volcano Big Ben, which, being snow covered and glaciated, reminded Mawson of Mt Erebus. The island was infamous for its bad weather and poor landing places, and because of this it was decided to land a shore party for nine days rather than risk daily landings. Davis and Mawson were still not on good terms, and relations soured further when Davis refused to move the ship closer to the shore party at Atlas Cove, forcing Mawson to make long and dangerous trips in the ship's launch. Others with more experience in small boats could have undertaken these runs in the launch, but Mawson invariably felt that when risks were involved, he as leader should step forward. Perhaps he felt this imperative even more strongly after the deaths of Ninnis and Mertz, even a decade and a half later. On the second of these trips the launch was nearly smashed to pieces on cliffs when the engine stalled.

From Heard Island the ship headed to Antarctica proper. For two long weeks they were frustrated by heavy pack-ice and fog, but on 31 December they had

Menu text within image:

DINER 22ᵈᵉᶜ 1929
Hors Doeuvres Varié
Potage Rosella ...
Saumon Sailor...
...sauce Robert
Asperge au Beurre
Jambon à l'Angleterre
Épinards ...
Pingouin Empereur à
...l'Antarcique
Sauce piquant....
Petit pois ... Pommes de terre rôti
Pouding Noël – Ellis
Sauce Cognac ...
Gelée - pâté d'émincé
..Dessert..
Café ..
Yalumba Four Crown
Dewars Special Vat
Embassy Cigars - Cigarettes
Dinner music by H.M.V. Artists

LAT 66°35'S
LONG 73°00'E

British
Australian
New Zealand
Antarctic
Research
Exp...

DISCOVERY
CHRISTMAS
1929

Frank Hurley was famous for his dark-room creations, such as this menu from the first BANZARE voyage. Such efforts helped off-set the fact that many of the pleasures of life were not present on board. However, the smiling faces of Mawson, the expedition commander (top), and Davis, Ship's Captain (bottom), belied their constant frustrations with each other, with Mawson wanting to push harder through the pack-ice to get to land while Davis was always worried about the ship's safety.

Only in ideal conditions could the Gypsy Moth be swung off the deck and lowered to the sea. Smooth conditions were required for take-off, and in a big swell there was danger of the aircraft smashing against the side of the ship. Once the aircraft was seriously damaged when being taken out of the water while carrying Mawson and pilot Eric Douglas.

sufficient open water and good enough visibility to lower their Gypsy Moth seaplane overboard. Two pilots, Stuart Campbell and Eric Douglas, were on board. The maiden flight revealed nothing but pack-ice in all directions, slightly less dense to the west and the north. Use of aircraft for aerial reconnaissance had been Mawson's aim in 1911, until the Vickers monoplane crashed in Adelaide and was converted to an air tractor. Aircraft were more sophisticated in 1929, but even so the idea of using a seaplane on BANZARE was ambitious, because the expedition was headed for the world's roughest oceans, which surrounded a continent that was home to the world's strongest winds, as Mawson's previous expedition had proven.

If Mawson had failed with aircraft in 1911, he had succeeded to some extent with the wireless. It was a sign of changing times was that the ship now had a wireless on board, to send and receive messages. although reception was still not always possible.

On 5 January 1930, chief pilot Stuart Campbell took Mawson up in the seaplane to get a clearer view of land still inaccessible because of pack-ice. Mawson called it Mac-Robertson Land, after the expedition's major sponsor, MacPherson Robertson, a Melbourne chocolate millionaire who donated £20,000 to the BANZARE's two voyages. The first landing was made on 13 January on what was called Proclamation Island – at 66°20'S, 47°E – off the coast of Enderby Land. Three months after leaving Cape Town the flag was finally planted. As fate would have it,

Proclamation Island from the air. The large body of water where Discovery *waits surrounded by pack-ice provided perfect conditions for the seaplane to take off. This photo is interesting because it shows how the pack-ice presented an impenetrable barrier to* Discovery. *Today's icebreakers would simply set a course for the island and force their way through the ice.*

On 13 January, three months after leaving Cape Town, it was a big relief for Mawson to get ashore and take possession of a portion of Antarctica for the Crown, even though in this case the landing was only on an island, Proclamation Island.

the following day *Norvegia* came into view, and Captain Riiser-Larsen boarded *Discovery*. The Norwegians also had aircraft, two of them, and had used one to land on the sea-ice of the continent and ski inland for eight kilometres. Mawson and Riiser-Larsen amicably agreed to explore different sectors, with *Discovery* staying to the east of the 40° East meridian and Norvegia remaining to the west.

However, the explorations of the remainder of the first BANZARE voyage were limited to trying to find a way through the pack-ice and carrying out some aerial surveys. On a flight on 25 January, back in the region of Proclamation Island, Campbell flew Mawson over the continent. Mawson wrote of this flight:

'I passed Campbell the flag attached to [a] mast and he stalled the engine and passed [it] over side. I retained the Proclamation, claiming once more all the land discovered and this time including the newly discovered slice at our farthest west.'

On 27 January, in an effort to confirm the existence of Knox Land, sighted by Wilkes in 1840, Eric Douglas took off with Mawson in difficult conditions. They saw only ice, and then were forced to bring the plane down in even rougher seas. As the seaplane was hoisted back onto *Discovery*, it smashed against the hull and almost sank. Mawson hung from underneath it with his feet trailing in the water, but his main worry was the plane, not himself. Meanwhile, MacKenzie, the First Officer, who was watching, was worried about the men, the seaplane and ship. He feared a catastrophic fire because the plane's fuel tank had split and emptied its contents. Eventually the damaged plane and the wet and shaken men were safely brought on board, and the plane repaired and test-flown on 6 February.

With the second BANZARE voyage planning to explore the coastline south of Australia, Discovery *departed from Hobart, not Cape Town. Here crowds are seen farewelling the ship on 22 November 1930. Among them was Lady Mawson, who had come to Hobart to enjoy the final busy days before her husband departed on what would be his last Antarctic voyage.*

The day after the accident, in seas that had not been sailed across before, they discovered an ice-covered island which Mawson named Bowman Island, after Isaiah Bowman, director of the American Geographical Society, who had helped raise funds for the expedition.

Davis was concerned about coal consumption and insisted that they return north to Kerguelen, which they did, arriving there with 50 tonnes spare. Davis has been criticised for this decision but he felt he needed a safety margin in case Discovery had to burn large amounts of coal by motoring through heavy pack-ice. The ship re-coaled at Kerguelen then a course was set east for Australia. Marine and meteorological surveys were conducted on the home voyage, as Mawson was never one to waste a moment or an opportunity. The ship arrived in Port Adelaide on 1 April 1930.

Although the expedition was hailed as a success, when the ship docked at Port Adelaide, Mawson was privately disappointed with the expedition's achievements. Scientifically they had gathered much new data, but as a man of the earth who liked

The brash ice shown here provided no major obstacle for Discovery, *although the ship did have to travel more slowly through brash than open seas. To the left is a tabular iceberg formed when the seaward end of a glacier calved off and floated north away from the continent.*

Using the natural lighting of the midnight sun, Hurley took this photo on Discovery of Sir Douglas Mawson (left) and the Norwegian Captain Riimer-Larsen. Their meeting was an amicable but serious affair, as both were representing the interests of their countries. They agreed that Mawson would explore to the east of 40° East, and Larsen to the west of this meridian. Meanwhile, two of the young Australian research staff shaved off their 'forest-like beards' which they had worn from Cape Town, disguised themselves in flying suits (which is what Riimer-Larsen wore on board) and 'were escorted around the engine-room as distinguished Norwegians by the unsuspecting chief officer.'

to hear the crunch of snow or rocks under his feet, he felt that their success in making land claims was very limited. However, from a political point of view the voyage was effective, with the expedition giving Britain satisfactory grounds for negotiating with the Norwegians.

During the absence of Mawson and the other members of the expedition, the Great Depression had taken hold and Mawson, who hoped to make up for the first voyage's failures with great successes on the second, was worried that government support would be withdrawn. This didn't happen, and although Australians had less money to spare for chocolates, Macpherson Robertson again sponsored BANZARE, raising his £14,000 contribution by £6,000. He was obviously pleased to have part of the continent named after him.

The second voyage was scheduled to leave from Tasmania. This time J.K. Davis was not on board, as he did not want to spend another summer arguing about *Discovery*'s capabilities and quantities of coal. Paquita was in Hobart to farewell the ship, which left Hobart on 22 November 1930. This time it was under the command of K.N. MacKenzie, First Officer on the first voyage. Mawson was still Commander

Mawson had arranged that Discovery *would re-coal from the huge modern whaling factory-ship,* James Clark Ross. *The bodies of the dead whales acted as buffers between the very well-appointed* Ross *and the 30-year-old* Discovery. *The contrast between the two vessels illustrated the amount of money that was being made from whaling, a pointed reminder of the need for the commercial rights to Antarctic resources to be defined and regulated.*

Hurley delighted in being high in the rigging with his camera, and on occasion was the first person to sight land. In this shot from the bowsprit taken off the Adelie Land Coast, 7 January 1931, Hurley shows Discovery *in open water approaching pack-ice, with the open water finishing abruptly at the 'brash ice margin'. The floating ice-fragments known as brash have been swept towards the pack ice in the background by the wind; if the wind were to die down, the brash would drift out into the open water and the distinct line between brash and open sea would disappear.*

The A.A.E.'s Main Base hut at Cape Denison was a desolate sight indeed when Discovery anchored off shore on 5 January 1931 and a party went ashore. Mawson and five others stayed ashore for the night, an experience that must have called up both grand and terrible memories of the expedition almost 20 years earlier. The fierce winds had caused some damage, but the major structures were remarkably intact.

Mawson (front) and Campbell in the Gypsy Moth as it is swung overboard. When Mawson mentioned the flights in his diary he recorded only what he saw and what the weather was like. However, every flight must have been an exciting experience because these were among the first to be made in Antarctica – the most impressive being Admiral Byrd's 1929 flight over the South Pole.

On 27 December 1930, Mawson wrote '...heavy pack on all sides barring progress to such an extent that it was decided to retrace our steps and regain open water and endeavour to find more westerly passage to the south'. Such conditions plagued both BANZARE voyages and led to a constant state of tension between Mawson and successive captains of Discovery.

of the expedition. First stop was Macquarie Island, then the ship searched fruitlessly for the Royal Company and Emerald Islands which had been named by whalers. The islands are now known not to exist.

After the Discovery's previous voyage was cut short by Captain Davis' concern about the limited coal on board, Mawson had arranged to re-coal this time from the Norwegian whaling ship, James Clark Ross. It took the expedition a few more days than planned to find the whaler, which had moved on from the rendezvous point, which meant some of the valuable coal loaded was used covering the extra distance in both directions. Mawson didn't let this annoyance colour his favourable impression of the size and the facilities of this modern vessel, though it was quite a contrast to the ancient Discovery. Both Mawson and MacKenzie dined with the Norwegian captain and his officers, and while Discovery took on 100 tonnes of coal and 25 of fresh water, they also accepted the invitation to have hot baths.

Then it was back to the realities of polar exploration. Heavy pack-ice prevented them from reaching the spectacular Balleny Islands, and in fact they were unable to land anywhere before Commonwealth Bay. On 29 December they encountered Kosmos, another Norwegian whaling mother-ship, which offered them 50 tonnes of coal. Mawson accepted and the transfer took place, with Discovery slightly damaged in the process. Captain MacKenzie was reported as saying he 'wouldn't go alongside a 20,000 tonner again in such a swell for 50 tons of gold, let alone coal'.

On 4 January 1931, they anchored off Cape Denison and went ashore. It must have been an emotional time for Mawson, who had experienced so much at this place. But as usual, he reported on the physical nature of things rather than his feelings.

At one of their landings, pilot Eric Douglas entertained Adelie penguins with the expedition gramophone. With no large land predators to fear, penguins are curious enough about humans without this

The abundance of pack-ice was a constant frustration during both BANZARE voyages, severely limiting access to the coast. Sometimes the floes were large enough for the men to walk upon to stretch their legs — or take photographs, such as this shot of Discovery *off the coast of Prince Elizabeth Land.*

Mawson named their last landing point on the second BANZARE voyage after Prime Minister Stanley Bruce, who had provided him with his official instructions 'to plant the British flag wherever you find it practicable to do so.' Bruce also provided clear instructions about where to put the proclamation (two copies required) in relation to the flagstaff. Mawson followed these instructions for the final time at Cape Bruce in Mac-Robertson Land, a region south of the Indian Ocean.

The image of Mawson wearing a balaclava in this team photo has been enlarged and reproduced in many places, most famously on the Australian $100 bill. The image has appeared in almost every book and photographic article about Mawson because there are no other portrait shots of him looking like an explorer, the role for which he is most famous. To Mawson's right is Captain K.N. MacKenzie, and squatting in front of Mawson with a white hat and scarf is Frank Hurley, who set up the photograph on Discovery *during the second BANZARE voyage.*

'I was greatly interested in examining our old living hut which, it was surprising to find, had withstood twenty years of ceaseless violent wind. Remarkable evidence of snow-blast erosion were everywhere evidenced on the exposed timbers. In many places the planks had thus been reduced in thickness by more than half an inch.'

Outside, on Azimuth Hill, one arm of the memorial cross to Ninnis and Mertz had been snapped off by the winds.

Mawson raised the flag, and claimed formal possession of King George V Land. He had been refused these powers in 1912 by the British government but had performed the ceremony anyway. Mawson and five members of the scientific staff stayed ashore for the night, then on 6 January Discovery continued its voyage to the west.

Flights in the Gypsy Moth enabled the long sections of the coast beyond the pack-ice to be roughly charted. On one of these flights Mawson confirmed the existence of Sabrina Land, which had been sighted by Balleny in 1839.

As *Discovery* travelled west, the expedition members saw many Norwegian whaling ships, which only increased Mawson's zeal to make more landings on the continent. MacKenzie was a much less experienced polar sailor than Captain Davis, and he frequently took the cautious option. Like Davis before him, MacKenzie was reluctant to follow Mawson's advice about how the ship could be taken through the pack-ice. Although Mawson rues this situation in his diary, they eventually achieved much more than the first BANZARE voyage.

On 13 February, they were able to come close to the shore of Mac-Robertson Land. They approached the dramatic rock peak of Murray Monolith in the ship's launch but were unable to land. Instead, as Mawson claimed the region for the King, the crew touched the rock with an oar. Perhaps Mawson was inspired to make this move by the memory of his own knighthood. A sealed canister was thrown ashore but it rolled down into the sea, so they retrieved it and threw it to higher ground, where it lodged. The ceremony was witnessed by 300,000 Adelie penguins, according to the estimate of New Zealand biologist Robert Falla.

Having farewelled Discovery *on its departure from Hobart, Paquita also met the ship on its return. One of the sailors presented her with a kitten, one of the offspring of the ship's cats, Nigger and Tiger, which became a much-loved Mawson family pet.*

The same day a more satisfactory ceremony was conducted at Scullin Monolith, where the shore party found a safe landing place. Mawson had time to collect some geological specimens, 'rocks' as he called them, before heading back to the ship.

On 18 February they made their final land-claiming proclamation at Cape Bruce, named after the same Prime Minister who had been reluctant to make public the primary purpose of the BANZARE expeditions. They landed, only to find themselves on a island a short distance from the mainland. When it came to proclamations, much more value was accorded to those made on the continent, so they spent another half an hour searching for a landing place on the mainland. The ceremony was performed and photographed on the Antarctic continent, then it was time to board the ship.

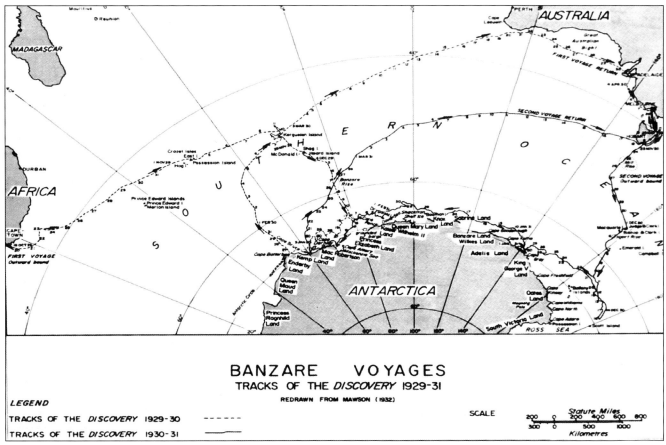

BANZARE   VOYAGES
TRACKS OF THE *DISCOVERY* 1929-31
REDRAWN FROM MAWSON (1932)

LEGEND

TRACKS OF THE *DISCOVERY* 1929-30   - - - - - -

TRACKS OF THE *DISCOVERY* 1930-31   ————

SCALE

The weather was good, and the coastline in the immediate area offered more possibilities for on-land exploration than anywhere else they had visited on the voyage. All the scientific staff, not only Mawson, were itching to spend more time ashore. However, MacKenzie was anxious to begin the return journey, and he had an arrangement with Mawson that when they were down to 100 tonnes of coal the ship would head for home. At Cape Bruce MacKenzie declared that this amount had been reached, and so, as agreed, a course was set for Hobart.

Mawson had calculated that 100 tonnes of coal would be just enough for the journey home, and he set this as the minimum because he always liked to push to the limit of what was possible. However, MacKenzie wanted a greater margin of safety, and he led Mawson to believe that the limit of the possible had been reached, while in fact he had a secret stash of extra coal. The Captain's scheme backfired, though, for as they motored eastward, the scientific staff became aware that the coal supply seemed to be self-replenishing. MacKenzie incurred the wrath not only of Mawson but of the scientific staff as well. He apologised, but was clearly pleased to disembark from ***Discovery*** when it arrived in Hobart on 19 March 1931. Despite this somewhat abbreviated second journey, Mawson felt well satisfied with the total achievements of the two voyages, in both political and scientific spheres.

The route of Discovery *on both voyages. Prepared by Mawson and first published in the Geographic Journal, August 1932, before Grenfell Price used it in his book and scientific report in the 1960s. The map is based on the version modified for the Jacka's edited* Mawson's Antarctic Diaries *in 1988. It was based on the work of the officers and expeditioners, particularly cartographers M.H. Moyes, RAN, and A.L. Kennedy, who were both on only one voyages and had previously been expeditioners on the A.A.E.*

205

CHAPTER 10

Man *of* Science

In photographs invariably Mawson looks
happier if he's sharing the ordeal with others.
Despite a lifetime of being photographed, it
appears that Mawson never learnt to enjoy the
process. This is one of his last formal portraits,
taken in the 1950s.

It was no coincidence that Mawson had conflicts with the captains on both BANZARE voyages. The exploration of uncharted Antarctic waters was a dangerous business. Pack-ice could hide submerged rocks, and a change in wind could trap the ship in the pack and even crush it. On both voyages they'd had constant difficulties in reaching or even sighting land because of the ice and the weather. For both captains the first priority had been the ship's safety, whereas Mawson's priority was to push just a little bit harder towards whatever goal he had in mind. And Mawson maintained the pressure during the long voyages back to Australia, when his oceanographic and meteorological work affected the ship's operations. At this time there were big gaps in knowledge in these disciplines and Mawson had been keen to collect as much data as possible.

Not everything had gone as planned on the A.A.E., and Mawson applied the lessons learnt on that expedition to the running of BANZARE, as well as the large amount of scientific knowledge he had gained in the intervening 15 years. He was also wiser in the ways of the world when it came to politics and diplomacy, although at this stage of his life he tended to leave these practices to the experts.

On BANZARE, where the primary if secret purpose was to claim land for the British Crown, Mawson could not resist the opportunity to explore known islands where virtually no scientific work had been done, such as the French possessions in

The Coorong, a 145-kilometre long sand soil enclosing an equally long lagoon, was a favourite place for family camping holidays. In this photo taken by her sister, Patricia, Jessica has her arm around Paquita while her father, even when relaxing in the bush, is wearing a bow-tie.

Douglas and Paquita remained a striking couple lifelong. Here they are seen on the way to a garden party with an unknown companion, most probably during the 1930s.

the southern Indian Ocean. This tendency to insist on carrying out research at every opportunity did compromise the expedition's ability to explore the Antarctic coastline thoroughly because of the time and coal that was 'wasted', as Captain Davis put it. But Mawson learnt from the shortcomings of the first voyage and achieved much more on the second. The end result was that the BANZARE voyages managed to chart in rough fashion much of the coastline between 45°E and 180°E longitude. Without the Gypsy Moth for aerial surveys, only a fraction of this would have been accomplished, proving the seaplane to have been a wise investment indeed.

Back in Adelaide in April 1931, Mawson was determined to get on top of several important matters before heading to England to give his presentation about BANZARE to the Royal Geographical Society; such a visit was a professional obligation, particularly now that he was a Fellow of the Society. Meanwhile, he was kept busy with organising BANZARE specimens and preliminary reports, and with ongoing projects at the university. He made sure that he and his students got away on field trips, which from his point of view were the essential part of geology. Mawson's study area was vast, and on these trips he not only instructed his students but also added to his own knowledge and understanding. Every site visited provided new information to be fitted into the geological jigsaw he continued to assemble throughout his life.

Mawson also kept up momentum on the Antarctic front. He lobbied the government to establish an Antarctic research program, but in the hard economic and social times of the early 1930s he had no chance of success. He wrote a paper about BANZARE which was read at the RGS in March 1932, but he didn't give his own presentation to the Society until early the following year. While he was in London, a British Order of Council affirmed King George V's sovereign rights to a large part of Antarctica, and placed under the authority of the Commonwealth of Australia the region between the 45°E and 160°E meridians of East longitude, southwards of the latitude 60°S. Excluded was the thin wedge of Adelie Land, which was French territory. The Australian government passed the Acceptance Bill in August 1936; more than one-third of Antarctica was now directly under Australian control.

Although the passing of the Act was a formality, it was an important one for Mawson. He had faced many frustrations with the outcomes of his expeditions, both financial and because the world was in great turmoil in different ways after both of his major ventures. At such times Antarctica was the remotest place on Earth and attracted little attention or interest. Outside Australia, Mawson's epic sledge journey had been eclipsed by Robert Falcon Scott's more spectacular demise, all the more gripping because salvation had been so close, and because Scott's final days and hours were so eloquently recorded in his diary. Shackleton's later exploits put Sir Ernest in firm second place with the English-speaking world. Mawson was a more modest man not concerned about his ranking among polar explorers. Such matters were inconsequential compared with the deaths of Ninnis and Mertz, and in any case Mawson placed less value on symbols than on realities. And the reality was that due to his efforts and those of his companions, there was now a substantial body of scientific knowledge about Antarctica, and more than a third of the Antarctic continent was under Australia's control. When the Acceptance Bill was passed in 1936 Mawson was 54 years old. He was

Mawson was never more at home than when out in the bush with a geology hammer in his hand. A perfect geologist-in-the-field photo by student Reg Sprigg.

past the age of expeditioning, but his ambition of Australianising that part of the continent closest to Australia was now officially achieved and he was ready to hang up his burberries. He was quietly and justly proud of his contribution to these history-making events. With the pressures of expeditioning behind him, he was able to renew his friendship with John King Davis, who had played such an important role in these achievements.

In 1932 Mawson had been elected to a five-year term as the President of the Australian Association for the Advancement of Science. During his 1935 Presidential speech, he spoke of the economic value of Antarctica. He spoke of whaling and mining at a time when the world's perspective on environmental matters was quite different. He saw that 'as a winter-sports playground for diversion in summer, Antarctica would be a thrill for Australians. I see no reason to delay the despatch from our ports of modern liners on summer pleasure cruises amongst

'I think the first impression that nearly everyone had on first meeting this striking-looking man was one of friendliness; and this applied equally to first year students as to world-famous scientists,' wrote Arthur Alderman , who took this photo of his professor and fellow students in the field

Stuart Campbell, seen here with Paquita and Jessica around the pond in the garden at Jerbii, was a good friend of the Mawsons. Campbell had been chief pilot on BAN-ZARE and became first acting head of ANARE, thanks to Mawson's influence.

pack-ice'. In these thoughts about Antarctic tourism he was 50 years ahead of his time.

Mawson was not afraid of having grand ideas, nor of ideas that challenged the status quo. Mawson's scientific program on the A.A.E had been very ambitious, and although 18 reports were published, many more never saw the printed page. Even with BANZARE, which was well sponsored and had the support of the three governments involved, there is research that even today has not been published. Publication of the BANZARE reports was a continuous – if not always top priority – job during the remainder of his professional life, although unlike the A.A.E, Mawson was very much the overseer. Also unlike the A.A.E,

When his daughters were looking for their father at Harewood, Mawson called out "Here I am!" and appeared holding this window frame. This photo in the same pose was taken in the woolshed he was building on their rural property.

he was able to galvanise the scientists involved into more or less immediate action. His daughter Patricia helped with the editing, and wrote the report on nematodes. Sufficient government funding had been made available to produce most of the BANZARE reports, and there was no imminent world war nor second winter in Antarctica to distract the report writers from their duties. Much of the

Patricia and Jessica, seen here with their father and one of his students during a geology field trip. Although neither was studying geology, they enjoyed going bush with their father.

Even when visiting his daughter Patricia for a family picnic Mawson is impeccably dressed. Patricia and two of her children stand with Mawson on a tractor sledge in the process is of being towed by Patricia's husband Evor Thomas to the picnic site on the Thomas property, providing a different kind of sledging experience to the dog-powered Antarctic version of Mawson's youth.

delay in the release in the reports was due to the time taken to prepare the manuscripts for publication.

Mawson is remembered as a geologist, but in order to do the geological work that he wanted to do in Antarctica, he had to be a glaciologist, a physicist, a magnetician, an oceanographer, a biologist, a meteorologist, a navigator and a cartographer. Of course, he gathered around him men with these skills, but to maximise productivity he made sure he understood their areas of work and helped design suitable scientific projects. This interest in the work of his staff frustrated his colleagues at times, but it also inspired them.

As a break from work at the university, Mawson devoted his spare time to the development of Harewood. This was his favourite hobby, a place where there was always more to do than there was time to do it. In this way it echoed geology and the exploration of Antarctica.

During the 1930s and 1940s, Mawson remained focused on his geological work, and became increasingly involved with broader Antarctic issues. He felt it was particularly important, now that Australia had control of so much territory, that ongoing research projects be carried out. In particular, he pushed for a research base to be established and manned for at least ten years by a roster of scientists from

different Australian universities. He kept abreast of international Antarctic developments and made every effort to meet polar explorers and scientists who visited Australia. The Australian government was prodded into thinking about Antarctic matters by US territorial flag waving, if not actual planting, by the millionaire-turned-explorer-aviator, Lincoln Ellsworth, in January 1939. However, World War II put all such thoughts on hold.

During the World War II Mawson concentrated on his geology. Cecil Madigan, still his colleague in the university's geology department, was surprised to find himself called up for active service, as he was an Officer of the Reserve. Despite being 51, he went to New South Wales as Commanding Officer of the School of Military Engineering. This put more responsibility back on Mawson, who shared it with junior members of the department, including Arthur

Mawson, the geologist, is well captured in this photograph which appeared in the Adelaide Advertiser *around the time of the BANZARE voyages.*

Before the procession into a University of Adelaide graduation ceremony, Mawson in light gown stands with an unknown associate to his right, while behind without hat is Sir Kerr-Grant, Professor of Physics, and Registrar Brampton. [35]

Alderman, who was eventually to succeed him as Professor in 1953. During this period Paquita accompanied her husband on many field trips, as life at Brighton had become quieter since their daughters had married. This was merely a peaceful interval as both Patricia and Jessica soon had children, a total of seven, who enjoyed running around the large garden at Brighton.

When the war was over, Mawson again lobbied for the establishment of both research and commercial operations in Antarctica. Mawson had received government funding for his expeditions but he had always retained control. He had also been frustrated by government shortsightedness, such as the New Zealand government's inability to see value in the Lake Manapouri hydroelectric scheme on several occasions. The Australian government had paid no real attention to Antarctica since the Australian Antarctic Territory had been declared. Mawson believed it was logical for Antarctic research bases to pay for themselves. Research into feasible commercial operations would fund further research, both pure science and commercially orientated. He also believed that a government research program would be at the mercy of political whims, whereas a commercial operation would more easily endure such essentially meaningless storms. It was a proposal that would have succeeded in the United States, but it got nowhere in Australia.

Mawson is seen here at the christening of the ANARE launch MacPherson Robertson in Melbourne in November, 1957. He maintained an active interest in Antarctic matters, retaining his position on ANARE's Expedition Planning Committee until his death 11 months after his photo was taken. In the front row from left: Rt. Hon and Mrs (soon Lord and Lady) Casey, Mrs Norman Robertson, Mawson, Mr Norman Robertson and Dr Phillip Law.

After his retirement from the Chair of Geology at the University of Adelaide in 1954, at the age of seventy, Mawson maintained contact with his circle of university friends. Here he is seen at home with Sir Kerr Grant, who had been Professor of Physics.

R.G. Casey, previously Minister for External Affairs but now in opposition, who had a strong interest in Antarctica since BANZARE days, was the catalyst for what was to become ANARE (Australian National Research Expeditions). In January 1947, he organised a meeting for Mawson with representatives from External Affairs, CSIR (later to become CSIRO) as well as the Navy and Air Force. The name of the resulting committee, the Executive Committee on Exploration and Exploitation, indicates the focus on 'progress' as well as the different values held when environmental degradation was not yet an issue. After several meetings it was decided that a preliminary expedition would be sent south, and on Mawson's advice Stuart Campbell, chief pilot on BANZARE, was appointed leader. Bases were set up on Heard and Macquarie Islands. In January 1949, Campbell was succeeded as head of ANARE by Phillip Law, a move which wasn't supported by Mawson. However, Mawson and Law soon became good friends, and whenever Mawson was in Melbourne as a member of ANARE's Executive Planning Committee he had lunch or dinner with Law, and they discussed details of operations that were beyond the scope of the committee. Of course, with Mawson having his own firm ideas about how things should be done, and Law being equally strong-minded, they did not always agree. Law remained as head of ANARE until 1966. In 1953 the first permanent continental base was set up on a rocky coast in Mac-Robertson Land. It was named Mawson Station, but it was never to be seen by its namesake.

When Mawson turned 65 in 1947, it had already been agreed that he would retire at 70. One of his unachieved goals was the construction of a new geology building at the University of Adelaide. Ever since his arrival in South Australia in 1905 Mawson had lobbied the University Council to build an appropriate geology building. The Council admitted the need but there was always something more urgent. Adelaide was the closest city to the rich mineral resources of Broken Hill, and to the iron-ore deposits in South Australia, and to Mawson it seemed logical that the Geology Department should become one of the strongest departments within the university. By the late 1940s funds for a chair in Mining Geology had been pledged by mining companies, but the university was in the ludicrous position of not having a suitable building. With an engineering as well as a geology degree, Mawson was able to involve himself in the design of the building, with the help of the University Architect. At last, in January 1949, the building was begun. It was completed by

Mawson with Sir Hubert Wilkins. Wilkins was born in South Australia and attended the School of Mines before setting off to see the world. He settled in the United States, led an adventurous life and became a famous polar explorer. This photo was taken in Adelaide in February, 1958, the year both men died.

August 1952, when it was given the name Mawson Laboratories. When Mawson retired in December 1952, he became Emeritus Professor and retained a room in the building. For him retirement meant retiring from teaching. He knew he would never retire from his geological and Antarctic interests.

By this stage Mawson's health was failing. In April 1954, he had a heart attack and spent a month in hospital. Much weakened, he decided to sell Harewood, perhaps so he wouldn't be tempted to go there. He still found the strength to travel to Melbourne for some ANARE meetings.

Mawson valued science ahead of politics, so when two Russian research ships, *Lena* and *Ob*, docked in Adelaide on their way home from Antarctica in April 1956, Mawson invited the officers to dine at his house, and he showed them around Adelaide. In turn he was shown over the ships. He was very interested in their scientific work. The Russians had two research stations in Australian Antarctic Territory, a long distance inland, and yet during their visits to Australia the Russians were ignored by the Australian authorities. Mawson felt this was petty and inappropriate, and wrote saying as much to R.G. Casey.

After husband's death, Lady Mawson bequeathed his collection of Antarctic books and equipment to the University of Adelaide. Here Lady Mawson is seen with Sir Robert Menzies, Prime Minister of Australia, at the opening of the Mawson Antarctic Collection in the university's Geology Department on 15 April 1961.

His health continued to deteriorate during 1957 and 1958, although he did manage a journey to a Canberra meeting of ANARE's Executive Planning Committee. He had a slight stroke in September, and in early October he called Professor Arthur Alderman to his home to hand over some papers he had hoped to finish writing. He enjoyed spending part of the following Sunday, a perfect day, sitting out in the garden with friends. The next morning he had another stroke and lost consciousness. He died the following day, 14 October 1958.

On the morning of 15 October, Sir Robert Menzies, Prime Minister of Australia, rang Paquita, offering his sympathies, and asking if the family would agree to a Commonwealth State Funeral. Paquita accepted the offer, and the funeral took place on 16 October at St

Jude's Church, Brighton. Hundreds of mourners gathered in and outside the church, among them many prominent Australians. The coffin was draped with the same Blue Ensign Sir Douglas Mawson had used to claim Antarctic Territory for the British Crown. At a memorial service held at St Peter's Cathedral in Adelaide four days later, Reverend T.T. Reed, Bishop of Adelaide, spoke of Sir Douglas Mawson's qualities: 'Intellectual capacity, the power to endure hardship, courage, resource, and the power to make others love knowledge and the pursuit of knowledge.'

He was all this, but he was also a man who loved the physical world, who was driven by the need to experience it and to quantify it in the language he had learnt, the language of science. Many people consider science clinical and unromantic, which it may be, but that does not mean that scientists are, too. As Douglas wrote to Paquita from Commonwealth Bay, when at last they had arrived at the Antarctic continent and the great adventure lay before him:

'Can you not feel it, too, as I write – the quickening of the pulse, the awakening of the mind, the tension of every fibre – this joy?'

In the late 1940s, Mawson jokes with Billy Hughes, former prime minister of Australia. Perhaps he is extolling the virtues of the metric system, still two decades from being implemented in Australia. In 1919 Mawson had written to Prime Minister Hughes pressing for the adoption of the metric system, including the financial benefits of being able to supply manufactured tools and machinery to the South American market serviced by the now-defeated Germany.

ACKNOWLEDGEMENTS

The prospect of producing a book about Sir Douglas Mawson was daunting indeed, but I took comfort in the thought that the many photographs included would help convey the sense of time and place that is a challenge in any writing project but absolutely essential in a biography. The photos did let me off the hook to a certain extent, thanks to the hard work of two people — my wife Barbara Scanlan, whose historical perspective and enthusiastic scrutiny turned a collection of photos into a cohesive visual record of an inspiring life, and Mark Pharaoh, Curator of the Mawson Antarctic Collection in Adelaide. The book would not have been possible without Mark's commitment to the project. His familiarity with the many hundreds of photographs in the collection made Barbara's job of photo researcher much easier. Mark's knowledge and perceptions of Mawson made him a valuable sounding board for my theories about the great man. He also worked tirelessly to meet our many demands and our tight deadlines. My thanks also to Yvonne Routledge, Manager of the Mawson Antarctic Collection.

Special thanks for out of circulation photographs and information about Sir Douglas and his work are due to Jessica McEwin, Alun McEwin, Andrew McEwin, Gareth Thomas, Pamela Karran, Alan and Mary Kerr Grant, Peter Gill, David McGonigal, Nancy Flannery, David Branagan, Greg Mortimer and David Parer. Robert Headland of the Scott Polar Research Institute in Cambridge provided good advice in our search for photos, and our thanks also to Philippa Smith, Picture Library Manager at the Institute, who was able to supply a much needed image at short notice. Thanks also to the South Australian Museum, particularly to Simon Langsford and Director Dr Tim Flannery, to Photo Wise Imaging at the University of Sydney, and to Kevin Bell and Rene Wanless at the Australian Antarctic Division.

Finally, I would like to thank the team at Lansdowne. Deborah Nixon and Margie Seale invited me to write the book, and Deborah juggled the production schedule along the way to accommodate my nine-week expedition to the Himalaya and three-week trip to Antarctica. This made the production schedule very tight and put a great deal of pressure on project co-ordinator Clare Wallis, editor Sarah Shrubb, and Mark Thacker and his team at Big Cat Design. Our thanks to all these people – their combined efforts have put Barbara's and my material together in a form which we hope will inspire many thousands of readers with the life of Sir Douglas Mawson.

PICTURE CREDITS

The majority of the photographs used in this book are part of the Mawson Antarctic Collection, which is held in Trust by the University of Adelaide. The collection of Mawson's polar libary, personal papers, equipment and photographs is housed at the university's Waite Campus in the specially restored coach-house of historic Urrbrae House. Yvonne Routledge is Manager of Urrbrae House Historic Precinct, and Mark Pharaoh is Curator of the Mawson Antarctic Collection. Most of the remaining photos have been generously provided by the Mawson family, friends of the family and by David Parer.

MAWSON ANTARCTIC COLLECTION
The following images are all from the Mawson Collection. The references, in order, are page number, photographer and where possible, a catalogue number. Unless otherwise stated, photograph credits are: DM (Douglas Mawson), MF (Mawson Family), UN (unknown), FH (Frank Hurley), MC (Mawson Collection).

Chapter 1   12/MF; 14/UN; 15 (top)/UN; 15 (bottom)/UN; 17/UN; 18/UN; 19/DM; 20/UN; 21/UN; 22 University of Adelaide. Chapter 2   24/DM; 27/UN; 31/DM; 34/DM; 37/DM; 38–39/DM; 40/UN; 42/DM; 43/DM; 44/DM; 46/UN; 48–49/DM. Chapter 3 - 55/W. Smith ; 56 University of Sydney Archives; 57/MF; 58/UN; 61/UN; 62/UN; 64/UN; 65/UN; 66 Gray. Chapter 4   68/FH/C68; 69/FH/C68; 70/FH/54; 71/FH/H50; 72/FH/W180; 74/Sawyer/C325; 75/Hamilton/H286; 76/Blake/H419; 77/FH/H718; 78/FH/H711; 81/FH/H586; 82/FH/W19; 84/FH/H605; 85/FH/W85; 86/FH/W75. Chapter 5   88/FH/W88; 90/FH/W119; 91/FH/H687; 92/FH/W184; 93/FH/H89; 94/FH/H704; 95/FH/W101; 96 (top)/FH/W45; 96 (bottom)/FH/Q791; 97/Mertz/C320; 98/FH/W170; 100/FH/C99; 101/Moyes/Q146; 102/FH/W31; 103/Mertz/C226; 104/FH/H693; 105/FH/H703; 106/FH/W32; 107/FH/W152; 109/DM/C239; 110–11/FH/W83; 112/FH/W63; 113/FH/W87; 114 (top)/FH/H697; 114(bottom)/DM/Q552; 115/DM/H591; 116/McLean/Q697; 117/FH/W788. Chapter 6 118/FH/H166; 121/FH/H196; 122/FH/W71; 124/FH/H686; 125/FH; 127/Mertz/C20; 128/FH/H992; 130/McLean/Q719; 131/McLean/Q638; 132/Hoadley/H171; 133/FH/Q672; 134/Watson/P178; 135/FH/H685. Chapter 7   140/FH/H714; 142/UN; 143/Hoadley/H454; 144/Hoadley/H412; 145/Hoadley/H409; 146/Hoadley/H454; 147/Hamilton/H252; 148/Watson/P64; 149/Hoadley/H244; 150/Gillies/C142; 151/FH/W90; 152/FH/W48; 153/McLean/W44; 154 (top)/FH/H679; 154 (bottom)/FH/H696; 155/FH/H692; 156 (top)/Mertz/C207; 156 (bottom)/FH/H104; 157/FH/W35. Chapter 8   160/UN; 161/MC; 166/MF; 169/O'Brien/MC; 173/MF; 174/MC. Chapter 9   178/FH; 181/182/FH/WP38; 183 (top)/FH/R234; 183 (bottom)/FH/WP27; 184/FH/R886; 185/FH/R508; 186/FH/WP3; 187/FH/WP120; 188/FH/WP96; 191/FH/R178; 192 (top)/FH/R66; 192 (bottom)/FH/WP220; 193/Johnston/G632; 194–5/FH/FP55; 195/FH/R243; 196/FH/R687; 197/FH/WP231; 198/FH/R837; 199 (top)/FH/R589/90; 199 (bottom)/FH/R175; 200/FH/WP126; 201/FH/WP217; 202(top)/FH/ WP126; 202 (bottom)/FH/R790; 203/FH/WP230; 204/MF. Chapter 10 209/UN.

All maps provided by Mawson Collection – see captions for more information. Floor plan on p.108 originally printed in *Home of the Blizzard* by Douglas Mawson, published by Heinemann in 1915. Endpapers: The route of *Discovery* on the two voyages of the BANZARE. The original map was prepared under Mawson's supervision.

Title page photograph: Mawson entitled his book about his most famous expedition Home of the Blizzard. He and his team had to accept blizzards as a part of life at their base and during sledge journeys, unless the storms were fierce enough to threaten their lives or make navigation impossible. (MC) Front cover photograph, see p.13 for more information (MC). Back cover (top): see p.194–5 (MC) Back cover (bottom, left): see p. 198 (MC), middle: Douglas Mawson (MC), right: see p.122 (MC).

THE REMAINING IMAGES WERE KINDLY PROVIDED BY THE FOLLOWING:
Darren Centofanti – p.20 (bottom), 23 (bottom), 136, 137, 138. University of Sydney Archives p. 56, 164. The Scott Polar Research Institute Picture no. P83698 – p. 59. The Adelaide Advertiser, p.214. Jessica McEwin – p.23, 52, 57, 162, 163, 165, 167, 168, 176, 206, 211 (both), 213, 217, 219 Gareth Thomas – p. 158, 162, 171, 172, 180, 190, 200. Patricia Thomas – p. 208, 212 (both) The Australasian, Melbourne Neg. no. H785, p. 209
Reg Sprigg/David Parer Collection p. 210. Kerr-Grant family, p. 214, 216. Mawson Estate p. 213 Australian Antarctic Division, Neg no. 5629. Photograph by Alan Campbell-Drury © Commonwealth of Australia p.215.

BIBLIOGRAPHY

Alderman, A. R. The Development of Geology in South Australia in *Records of the Australian Academy of Science*. Vol 1. Number 1. Canberra December 1967.

Ayres, Philip. *Mawson, A Life*. Melbourne University Press, Melbourne 1999.

Bickel, Lennard. *This Accursed Land*. Macmillan, Melbourne 1977.

Chester, Jonathan. *Going to Extremes*. Doubleday, Sydney, 1986.

Davis, John King. *High Latitude*. Melbourne University Press, Melbourne 1962.

Crossley, Louise (ed), *Trial by Ice, The Antarctic Journals of John King Davis*. Erskine Press, 1997.

Fletcher, Harold. *Antarctic Days with Mawson*. Angus & Robertson, Sydney 1984.

Grenfell Price, A. *BANZARE Reports, Series A, Vol. 1, Geographical Report*, Adelaide, 1963.

Huntford, Roland. Shackleton. Hodder & Stoughton, London 1985.

Jacka, F. and Jacka, E. (eds), *Mawson's Antarctic Diaries*. Allen & Unwin Sydney 1988.

Laseron, Charles. *South with Mawson* Angus & Robertson, Sydney 1957 (2nd Edition).

Mackay, A. Forbes, *Diary of Forbes Mackay, 1908–1909*, Royal Scottish Museum Natural History March 1982.

MacLeod, Roy, 'Full Honour and Gain to Science': Munitions Production, Technical Intelligence and the Wartime Career of Sir Douglas Mawson, FRS. in *Historical Records of Australia Science*, Vol. 7 No.2.

Mawson, Douglas. *Home of the Blizzard*. Wakefield Press. Adelaide 1996.

Mawson, Paquita. *Mawson of the Antarctic*. Longmans, London 1964.

Mertz, Xavier. Antarctic diary held at Mawson Antarctic Collection, Adelaide.

Parer, David and Parer-Cook, Elizabeth. *Douglas Mawson, The Survivor*, Alella Books/Australian Broadcasting Corporation, Melbourne, 1983

Price, A. Grenfell. *BANZARE Reports – Series A, Vol. 1 Geographical Report*. Mawson Institute for Scientific Research, Adelaide 1963.

Reader's Digest. *Antarctica, Great Stories from the Frozen Continent*. Reader's Digest, Sydney 1985.

Scott, Robert Falcon. 'Scott's Last Expedition', Vol. I, Smith, Elder & Co. London 1913.

Swan, R.A., *Australia in the Antarctic*, Melbourne, 1961.

Savours, Ann. *The Voyages of the Discovery*. Virgin, London 1992.

Shackleton, E.H (ed) *Aurora Australis*, Bay Books, Sydney 1988.

Suzyumov, E.M., *A Life Given to the Antarctic*, English trans., T.T Glaessner, Adelaide, 1968.

Taylor, Griffith, *Douglas Mawson*, Melbourne, 1962.

Webb, Eric Magnetic Polar Journey 1912 unpublished personal account, 1965, P. Gill collection.

MAWSON QUOTATIONS

Quotes from Mawson in the first person have been reproduced with the kind permission of the publishers of the following books (see above for details): *Home of the Blizzard* (pages 82, 93, 123, 128–129, 129, 130, 133, 134, 142–43, 153, 154), *Mawson's Antarctic Diaries* (27–29, 39–40, 46, 47, 58, 104–106, 109, 125, 132, 146, 149) *BANZARE Report* (115, 189, 192, 200), *Mawson of the Antarctic* (53, 60, 67, 90, 102, 146, 219), *South with Mawson* (65, 92–93, 94), *Mawson, A Life* (23), *Scott's Last Expedition* (166) and Mertz's Diary (125–126, 126, 129).

INDEX

224